50 Kids Birthday Party Treat Recipes for Home

By: Kelly Johnson

Table of Contents

- Cupcakes
- Cake pops
- Rice crispy treats
- Chocolate-covered strawberries
- Mini pizzas
- Fruit skewers
- Popcorn balls
- Ice cream sandwiches
- Cookie decorating kits
- Mini sliders
- Mini hot dogs
- Mini tacos
- Cheese and crackers
- Mini grilled cheese sandwiches
- Veggie sticks with dip
- Mini donuts
- Fruit smoothies
- Rainbow fruit platter
- Chicken nuggets
- Macaroni and cheese bites
- Mini fruit pizzas
- Cheese quesadillas
- Pretzel rods dipped in chocolate
- Jello cups
- Mini muffins
- Fruit salad cups
- S'mores bites
- Cake batter popcorn
- Sandwich kabobs
- Mini fruit tarts
- Chocolate fondue with dippers
- Mini bagel pizzas
- Rainbow popcorn
- Yogurt parfait cups
- Mini chicken sliders

- Candy apples
- Mini corn dogs
- Rainbow grilled cheese sandwiches
- Marshmallow cereal bars
- Mini pancakes
- Cucumber sandwiches
- Mini spring rolls
- Brownie bites
- Taco cups
- Mini pretzels with cheese dip
- Edible cookie dough bites
- Cotton candy
- Veggie sushi rolls
- Chocolate chip cookie cups
- Jellybean popcorn

Cupcakes

Ingredients:

- 1 and 1/2 cups all-purpose flour
- 1 and 1/2 teaspoons baking powder
- 1/4 teaspoon salt
- 1/2 cup unsalted butter, softened
- 3/4 cup granulated sugar
- 2 large eggs, room temperature
- 1 teaspoon vanilla extract
- 1/2 cup milk

Instructions:

1. Preheat Oven and Prepare Muffin Pan:
    - Preheat your oven to 350°F (175°C). Line a muffin pan with cupcake liners.
2. Mix Dry Ingredients:
    - In a medium bowl, whisk together the flour, baking powder, and salt. Set aside.
3. Cream Butter and Sugar:
    - In a large bowl, beat the softened butter and granulated sugar together using a hand mixer or stand mixer until light and fluffy, about 2-3 minutes.
4. Add Eggs and Vanilla:
    - Add the eggs, one at a time, beating well after each addition. Mix in the vanilla extract.
5. Alternate Mixing Dry and Wet Ingredients:
    - Gradually add the dry ingredients to the butter mixture, alternating with the milk, beginning and ending with the dry ingredients. Mix until just combined, being careful not to overmix.
6. Fill Cupcake Liners:
    - Spoon the batter into the prepared cupcake liners, filling each about 2/3 full.
7. Bake:
    - Bake in the preheated oven for 18-20 minutes, or until a toothpick inserted into the center of a cupcake comes out clean.
8. Cool:
    - Remove the cupcakes from the muffin pan and transfer them to a wire rack to cool completely before frosting.

Frosting Ideas:

- Vanilla Buttercream Frosting:
    - Ingredients: 1/2 cup unsalted butter (softened), 2 cups powdered sugar, 1-2 tablespoons milk, 1 teaspoon vanilla extract.
    - Instructions: Beat butter until creamy. Gradually add powdered sugar, milk, and vanilla extract, beating until smooth and creamy.
- Chocolate Ganache:

- Ingredients: 1/2 cup heavy cream, 1 cup semi-sweet chocolate chips.
- Instructions: Heat heavy cream until just simmering, then pour over chocolate chips. Stir until smooth and glossy.
- Cream Cheese Frosting:
  - Ingredients: 1/2 cup unsalted butter (softened), 8 oz cream cheese (softened), 4 cups powdered sugar, 1 teaspoon vanilla extract.
  - Instructions: Beat butter and cream cheese until smooth. Gradually add powdered sugar and vanilla, beating until fluffy.

Enjoy these classic cupcakes with your favorite frosting for a delightful treat!

Cake pops

Ingredients:

- 1 box cake mix (flavor of your choice), plus ingredients listed on the box (typically eggs, oil, and water)
- 1 can frosting (flavor that complements your cake, such as vanilla or cream cheese)
- 12 oz candy melts or chocolate chips (for coating)
- Lollipop sticks
- Sprinkles or decorations (optional)

Instructions:

1. Bake the Cake:
    - Prepare and bake the cake according to the instructions on the box. Allow the cake to cool completely.
2. Crumble the Cake:
    - Once cooled, crumble the cake into fine crumbs using your hands or a fork.
3. Mix with Frosting:
    - Add about 3/4 of the can of frosting to the crumbled cake. Mix together until well combined and the mixture holds together when pressed. Add more frosting if needed.
4. Form Cake Balls:
    - Roll the cake mixture into small balls, about 1-2 inches in diameter, and place them on a baking sheet lined with parchment paper.
5. Insert Sticks:
    - Melt a small amount of candy melts or chocolate chips. Dip the tip of each lollipop stick into the melted chocolate and insert it into each cake ball, about halfway through. Place the baking sheet in the refrigerator for about 15-20 minutes to allow the cake balls to firm up around the sticks.
6. Coat with Chocolate:
    - Melt the remaining candy melts or chocolate chips in a microwave-safe bowl according to package instructions. Dip each cake pop into the melted chocolate, allowing any excess chocolate to drip off. You can gently tap the stick against the edge of the bowl to help remove excess chocolate.
7. Decorate:
    - While the chocolate coating is still wet, sprinkle with sprinkles or decorations if desired. Place the cake pops upright in a cake pop stand or styrofoam block to set.
8. Let Harden:
    - Allow the cake pops to harden completely at room temperature or in the refrigerator before serving.
9. Serve:
    - Once hardened, your cake pops are ready to be enjoyed! They make a fun and delicious treat for kids' birthday parties or any celebration.

Enjoy making and sharing these delightful cake pops with family and friends!

Rice crispy treats

Ingredients:

- 6 cups crispy rice cereal
- 4 cups mini marshmallows
- 3 tablespoons unsalted butter
- 1/2 teaspoon vanilla extract
- Pinch of salt (optional)

Instructions:

1. Prepare the Pan:
    - Grease a 9x13-inch baking dish with butter or cooking spray. Set aside.
2. Melt Butter and Marshmallows:
    - In a large pot, melt the butter over low heat. Add the mini marshmallows and stir continuously until completely melted and smooth. Stir in the vanilla extract and salt (if using).
3. Mix in Cereal:
    - Remove the pot from heat. Add the crispy rice cereal to the marshmallow mixture. Stir quickly until the cereal is evenly coated with the marshmallow mixture.
4. Press into Pan:
    - Transfer the mixture to the prepared baking dish. Use a greased spatula or wax paper to press the mixture evenly into the pan.
5. Let Cool:
    - Allow the rice crispy treats to cool and set at room temperature for about 30 minutes.
6. Cut and Serve:
    - Once cooled and firm, cut the treats into squares or rectangles using a sharp knife. Serve and enjoy!

Variations:

- Chocolate Rice Crispy Treats: Add 1/2 cup of melted chocolate chips to the marshmallow mixture before adding the cereal.
- Peanut Butter Rice Crispy Treats: Stir in 1/2 cup of creamy peanut butter with the marshmallows until smooth before adding the cereal.
- Fruity Rice Crispy Treats: Add 1/2 cup of dried fruit (such as chopped dried apricots or cranberries) to the cereal mixture for a fruity twist.

These rice crispy treats are quick and easy to make, perfect for kids' birthday parties or any occasion where a sweet, chewy treat is needed!

Chocolate-covered strawberries

Ingredients:

- Fresh strawberries (about 1 pound or 16-20 strawberries)
- 8 oz semi-sweet or dark chocolate, chopped (or chocolate chips)
- 1 tablespoon vegetable shortening or coconut oil (optional, for smoother chocolate)

Instructions:

1. Prepare the Strawberries:
    - Wash and thoroughly dry the strawberries. Line a baking sheet with parchment paper or wax paper.
2. Melt the Chocolate:
    - In a microwave-safe bowl or using a double boiler, melt the chocolate and vegetable shortening (if using), stirring frequently until smooth and completely melted.
3. Dip the Strawberries:
    - Hold each strawberry by the stem and dip it into the melted chocolate, swirling to coat evenly. Allow any excess chocolate to drip back into the bowl.
4. Set on Baking Sheet:
    - Place each chocolate-covered strawberry onto the prepared baking sheet. Repeat with the remaining strawberries.
5. Chill to Set:
    - Once all strawberries are dipped, refrigerate the baking sheet for about 30 minutes to allow the chocolate to set and harden.
6. Serve and Enjoy:
    - Remove the chocolate-covered strawberries from the refrigerator shortly before serving. They are best enjoyed fresh on the same day they are made.

Variations:

- White Chocolate Option: Substitute semi-sweet or dark chocolate with white chocolate for a different flavor profile.
- Decorations: Before the chocolate sets, sprinkle the strawberries with chopped nuts, coconut flakes, or drizzle with contrasting chocolate for a decorative touch.
- Gift Idea: Package chocolate-covered strawberries in a decorative box or wrap individually for a delightful gift.

Chocolate-covered strawberries are a delicious and elegant treat, perfect for celebrations, romantic occasions, or simply as a delightful dessert.

Mini pizzas

Ingredients:

- English muffins or small pizza crusts (about 4)
- 1/2 cup pizza sauce or marinara sauce
- 1 cup shredded mozzarella cheese
- Toppings of your choice (e.g., pepperoni, diced bell peppers, sliced mushrooms, olives, etc.)
- Italian seasoning or dried oregano (optional)
- Olive oil (optional, for drizzling)

Instructions:

1. Preheat Oven:
   - Preheat your oven to 375°F (190°C).
2. Prepare Pizza Crusts:
   - Split the English muffins in half or use small pre-made pizza crusts. Place them on a baking sheet lined with parchment paper.
3. Top with Sauce:
   - Spread about 1-2 tablespoons of pizza sauce or marinara sauce onto each pizza crust, leaving a small border around the edges.
4. Add Cheese and Toppings:
   - Sprinkle shredded mozzarella cheese evenly over the sauce. Add your desired toppings such as pepperoni, diced vegetables, or olives.
5. Bake:
   - Bake mini pizzas in the preheated oven for 10-12 minutes, or until the cheese is melted and bubbly, and the edges of the crust are golden brown.
6. Optional Finishing Touches:
   - If desired, sprinkle Italian seasoning or dried oregano over the hot mini pizzas before serving. Drizzle with a little olive oil for added flavor.
7. Serve:
   - Remove from the oven and let cool slightly before serving. Mini pizzas are great for parties, after-school snacks, or a quick dinner option.

Enjoy these mini pizzas fresh and customize them with your favorite toppings for a tasty treat!

Fruit skewers

Ingredients:

- Assorted fruits (such as strawberries, pineapple, grapes, melon, kiwi, and mango)
- Wooden or metal skewers

Optional:

- Honey or maple syrup, for drizzling
- Yogurt dip or chocolate sauce, for dipping

Instructions:

1. Prepare the Fruits:
   - Wash and dry all fruits thoroughly. Peel and slice fruits like pineapple, mango, and kiwi into bite-sized pieces. Remove stems from strawberries and slice larger fruits into chunks.
2. Assemble Skewers:
   - Thread the prepared fruit pieces onto wooden or metal skewers in any desired pattern. Leave a little space at the bottom of the skewer for easy handling.
3. Optional Drizzle:
   - If desired, drizzle honey or maple syrup over the assembled fruit skewers for added sweetness.
4. Serve:
   - Arrange the fruit skewers on a serving platter or display them upright in a tall glass or vase for an attractive presentation.
5. Optional Dip:
   - Serve fruit skewers with a side of yogurt dip or chocolate sauce for dipping, if desired.

Tips:

- Use a variety of colorful fruits to make the skewers visually appealing.
- Soak wooden skewers in water for 30 minutes before threading the fruit to prevent them from burning during grilling or baking.
- Get creative with different fruit combinations and alternate them on the skewers for variety.

Fruit skewers are a refreshing and healthy snack or dessert option, perfect for parties, gatherings, or simply enjoying on a sunny day.

Popcorn balls

Ingredients:

- 10 cups popped popcorn (about 1/2 cup unpopped kernels)
- 1/2 cup unsalted butter
- 1 package (10 oz) marshmallows (about 40 marshmallows)
- 1 teaspoon vanilla extract
- 1/2 teaspoon salt
- Optional: Food coloring, candy pieces, sprinkles, or other decorations

Instructions:

1. Prepare Popcorn:
   - Pop the popcorn using an air popper or stovetop method. Remove any unpopped kernels and place the popped popcorn in a large mixing bowl.
2. Melt Butter and Marshmallows:
   - In a large pot, melt the butter over medium heat. Add the marshmallows and stir continuously until completely melted and smooth. Stir in the vanilla extract and salt.
3. Coat Popcorn:
   - Pour the melted marshmallow mixture over the popped popcorn in the bowl. Use a greased spatula or wooden spoon to gently fold and coat the popcorn evenly with the marshmallow mixture.
4. Shape into Balls:
   - Grease your hands with butter or cooking spray to prevent sticking. Working quickly while the mixture is still warm, shape the coated popcorn into balls, pressing firmly to compact them. You can use an ice cream scoop or your hands to portion the mixture.
5. Decorate (Optional):
   - If desired, decorate the popcorn balls with food coloring, candy pieces, sprinkles, or other decorations before they set completely. Press the decorations gently into the surface of the popcorn balls.
6. Let Cool and Set:
   - Place the shaped popcorn balls on a parchment-lined baking sheet or in muffin tin cups to hold their shape. Allow them to cool and set at room temperature for about 30 minutes to 1 hour.
7. Serve or Store:
   - Once cooled and set, the popcorn balls are ready to be enjoyed! Serve them immediately or store them in an airtight container at room temperature for up to 3 days.

Variations:

- Chocolate Popcorn Balls: Stir in 1/2 cup of chocolate chips or cocoa powder into the melted marshmallow mixture for chocolate-flavored popcorn balls.
- Peanut Butter Popcorn Balls: Add 1/2 cup of peanut butter to the melted marshmallow mixture for peanut butter-flavored popcorn balls.
- Fruity Popcorn Balls: Mix in freeze-dried fruit pieces or flavored gelatin powder for fruity-flavored popcorn balls.

These homemade popcorn balls are a fun and nostalgic treat, perfect for parties, Halloween, or anytime you're craving a sweet and crunchy snack!

Ice cream sandwiches

Ingredients:

- 1 package (about 12) chocolate chip cookies or any other flavor cookies of your choice
- 2 cups of your favorite ice cream flavor, slightly softened

Optional Additions:

- Sprinkles
- Mini chocolate chips
- Chopped nuts
- Shredded coconut

Instructions:

1. Prepare Cookies:
    - If baking cookies from scratch, follow your favorite recipe and allow them to cool completely before assembling the ice cream sandwiches. If using store-bought cookies, ensure they are cooled to room temperature.
2. Slightly Soften Ice Cream:
    - Take the ice cream out of the freezer and let it sit at room temperature for about 5-10 minutes, or until it's slightly softened and easy to scoop.
3. Assemble Sandwiches:
    - Place a scoop of softened ice cream (about 1/4 to 1/3 cup) onto the bottom side of one cookie.
    - Take another cookie and gently press it down onto the ice cream, creating a sandwich.
    - Use a spatula or the back of a spoon to smooth out the edges of the ice cream.
    - Repeat with the remaining cookies and ice cream.
4. Optional Decorations:
    - If desired, roll the edges of the ice cream sandwiches in sprinkles, mini chocolate chips, chopped nuts, or shredded coconut for added decoration and flavor.
5. Freeze:
    - Once assembled, place the ice cream sandwiches on a baking sheet lined with parchment paper or a silicone mat.
    - Transfer the baking sheet to the freezer and freeze the sandwiches for at least 1-2 hours, or until the ice cream is firm.
6. Serve:
    - Remove the ice cream sandwiches from the freezer and let them sit at room temperature for a few minutes before serving to soften slightly.
    - Enjoy these delicious homemade ice cream sandwiches as a refreshing treat on a hot day or as a delightful dessert for any occasion!

Note:

- You can customize your ice cream sandwiches by using different cookie flavors and ice cream combinations. Get creative with your favorite cookie and ice cream flavors to create unique and delicious combinations!

Cookie decorating kits

Ingredients:

- 1 package (about 12) chocolate chip cookies or any other flavor cookies of your choice
- 2 cups of your favorite ice cream flavor, slightly softened

Optional Additions:

- Sprinkles
- Mini chocolate chips
- Chopped nuts
- Shredded coconut

Instructions:

1. Prepare Cookies:
    - If baking cookies from scratch, follow your favorite recipe and allow them to cool completely before assembling the ice cream sandwiches. If using store-bought cookies, ensure they are cooled to room temperature.
2. Slightly Soften Ice Cream:
    - Take the ice cream out of the freezer and let it sit at room temperature for about 5-10 minutes, or until it's slightly softened and easy to scoop.
3. Assemble Sandwiches:
    - Place a scoop of softened ice cream (about 1/4 to 1/3 cup) onto the bottom side of one cookie.
    - Take another cookie and gently press it down onto the ice cream, creating a sandwich.
    - Use a spatula or the back of a spoon to smooth out the edges of the ice cream.
    - Repeat with the remaining cookies and ice cream.
4. Optional Decorations:
    - If desired, roll the edges of the ice cream sandwiches in sprinkles, mini chocolate chips, chopped nuts, or shredded coconut for added decoration and flavor.
5. Freeze:
    - Once assembled, place the ice cream sandwiches on a baking sheet lined with parchment paper or a silicone mat.
    - Transfer the baking sheet to the freezer and freeze the sandwiches for at least 1-2 hours, or until the ice cream is firm.
6. Serve:
    - Remove the ice cream sandwiches from the freezer and let them sit at room temperature for a few minutes before serving to soften slightly.
    - Enjoy these delicious homemade ice cream sandwiches as a refreshing treat on a hot day or as a delightful dessert for any occasion!

Note:

- You can customize your ice cream sandwiches by using different cookie flavors and ice cream combinations. Get creative with your favorite cookie and ice cream flavors to create unique and delicious combinations!

Mini sliders

Ingredients:

- 1 pound ground beef (or your choice of ground meat)
- Salt and pepper, to taste
- Slider buns or dinner rolls
- Cheese slices (optional)
- Lettuce leaves
- Tomato slices
- Pickles
- Condiments of your choice (such as ketchup, mustard, mayonnaise)

Instructions:

1. Form Patties:
    - Divide the ground beef into small portions, about 2-3 tablespoons each. Shape them into mini patties slightly larger than the size of your slider buns. Season both sides of the patties with salt and pepper.
2. Cook Patties:
    - Heat a skillet or grill pan over medium-high heat. Cook the mini patties for about 2-3 minutes on each side, or until they are cooked through to your desired level of doneness. If adding cheese, place a slice of cheese on top of each patty during the last minute of cooking to melt.
3. Assemble Sliders:
    - Slice the slider buns or dinner rolls in half horizontally. Place a lettuce leaf and tomato slice on the bottom half of each bun. Add a cooked patty on top of the tomato.
4. Add Toppings:
    - Place a pickle slice on top of the patty. Add any additional condiments of your choice, such as ketchup, mustard, or mayonnaise.
5. Serve:
    - Place the top half of the slider buns on each assembled slider. Secure them with toothpicks if necessary. Serve the mini sliders immediately while warm.

Variations:

- Cheeseburger Sliders: Add a slice of cheese to each patty during cooking for classic cheeseburger sliders.
- Bacon Sliders: Cook bacon until crispy and place a piece on top of each patty before assembling the sliders.
- Veggie Sliders: Replace the ground beef with a veggie patty or grilled portobello mushroom for vegetarian-friendly sliders.

These mini sliders are perfect for parties, game day gatherings, or a fun weeknight dinner for the family. Customize them with your favorite toppings and enjoy their deliciousness in every bite!

Mini hot dogs

Ingredients:

- Cocktail sausages or mini hot dogs
- Mini hot dog buns or small dinner rolls
- Ketchup
- Mustard
- Relish (optional)
- Grated cheese (optional)
- Diced onions (optional)

Instructions:

1. Cook the Sausages:
    - Preheat a skillet or grill pan over medium heat. Add the cocktail sausages or mini hot dogs to the skillet and cook, turning occasionally, until they are heated through and lightly browned on all sides. This usually takes about 5-7 minutes.
2. Prepare the Buns:
    - While the sausages are cooking, prepare the mini hot dog buns or small dinner rolls. Slice each bun horizontally, making sure not to cut all the way through.
3. Assemble the Mini Hot Dogs:
    - Place a cooked sausage or mini hot dog inside each bun.
4. Add Condiments and Toppings:
    - Add your desired condiments and toppings to the mini hot dogs. Classic options include ketchup, mustard, and relish. You can also sprinkle grated cheese or diced onions on top if desired.
5. Serve:
    - Arrange the assembled mini hot dogs on a platter and serve them immediately. You can secure each mini hot dog with a toothpick if needed.

Variations:

- Pigs in a Blanket: Wrap each cocktail sausage or mini hot dog in a strip of crescent roll dough and bake them in the oven according to the package instructions for a fun twist.
- Chili Cheese Dogs: Top each mini hot dog with chili con carne and shredded cheese for a hearty and flavorful option.
- Buffalo Hot Dogs: Toss the cooked mini hot dogs in buffalo sauce and serve them with blue cheese dressing and celery sticks for a spicy kick.

These mini hot dogs are perfect for parties, game day snacks, or anytime you're craving a fun and delicious bite-sized treat! Adjust the toppings to suit your preferences and enjoy.

Mini tacos

Ingredients:

- Mini taco shells (or regular taco shells, broken into smaller pieces)
- Ground beef or chicken
- Taco seasoning mix
- Shredded lettuce
- Diced tomatoes
- Shredded cheese (such as cheddar or Mexican blend)
- Sour cream
- Sliced jalapeños (optional)
- Chopped cilantro (optional)
- Salsa (optional)

Instructions:

1. Prepare the Taco Filling:
    - In a skillet over medium heat, cook the ground beef or chicken until browned and cooked through. Drain any excess fat. Add the taco seasoning mix and water according to the package instructions. Stir well and simmer for a few minutes until the mixture thickens.
2. Assemble the Mini Tacos:
    - Fill each mini taco shell with a spoonful of the prepared taco meat.
3. Add Toppings:
    - Top the mini tacos with shredded lettuce, diced tomatoes, shredded cheese, sour cream, sliced jalapeños, chopped cilantro, and salsa, according to your preference.
4. Serve:
    - Arrange the assembled mini tacos on a platter and serve them immediately. You can also set up a taco bar with various toppings and let your guests customize their mini tacos.

Variations:

- Vegetarian Mini Tacos: Substitute the ground meat with cooked black beans, refried beans, or sautéed vegetables such as bell peppers, onions, and mushrooms.
- Fish or Shrimp Mini Tacos: Use grilled or sautéed fish or shrimp as the filling for a seafood twist on mini tacos.
- Breakfast Mini Tacos: Fill mini taco shells with scrambled eggs, cooked breakfast sausage or bacon, shredded cheese, and salsa for a delicious breakfast option.

These mini tacos are perfect for parties, gatherings, or as a fun and bite-sized meal option for taco night. Customize them with your favorite toppings and enjoy!

Cheese and crackers

Ingredients:

- Assorted cheeses (such as cheddar, Swiss, brie, gouda, or goat cheese)
- Crackers (such as water crackers, whole grain crackers, or multigrain crackers)
- Grapes or berries (for garnish)
- Nuts (such as almonds, walnuts, or cashews)
- Honey or fruit preserves (optional, for drizzling)
- Fresh herbs (such as rosemary or thyme, for garnish)

Instructions:

1. Select Cheeses:
    - Choose a variety of cheeses with different textures and flavors to create a diverse cheese platter. Arrange them on a large serving board or platter.
2. Prepare Crackers:
    - Arrange an assortment of crackers around the cheeses on the serving board. You can use a combination of plain and flavored crackers for variety.
3. Garnish with Fruit:
    - Place clusters of grapes or berries around the cheese and crackers for a pop of color and freshness.
4. Add Nuts:
    - Scatter a handful of nuts, such as almonds, walnuts, or cashews, around the cheese platter for extra crunch and texture.
5. Drizzle with Honey or Preserves (Optional):
    - If desired, drizzle honey or spoon fruit preserves over some of the cheeses for added sweetness and flavor contrast.
6. Garnish with Fresh Herbs:
    - Sprinkle fresh herbs, such as rosemary or thyme leaves, over the cheese platter for a decorative touch and aroma.
7. Serve:
    - Place the cheese and crackers platter in the center of the table and invite guests to help themselves. Provide cheese knives and small plates for serving.

Variations:

- Charcuterie Addition: Enhance your cheese platter by adding cured meats, such as prosciutto, salami, or chorizo, for a charcuterie and cheese board.
- Dried Fruit: Include dried fruits, such as apricots, figs, or cranberries, for additional sweetness and texture.
- Crudités: Serve sliced vegetables, such as carrots, cucumbers, or bell peppers, alongside the cheese and crackers for a refreshing contrast.

This cheese and crackers platter is perfect for entertaining guests at parties, gatherings, or wine nights. Customize it with your favorite cheeses, crackers, and accompaniments for a delicious and elegant appetizer option.

Mini grilled cheese sandwiches

Ingredients:

- Assorted cheeses (such as cheddar, Swiss, brie, gouda, or goat cheese)
- Crackers (such as water crackers, whole grain crackers, or multigrain crackers)
- Grapes or berries (for garnish)
- Nuts (such as almonds, walnuts, or cashews)
- Honey or fruit preserves (optional, for drizzling)
- Fresh herbs (such as rosemary or thyme, for garnish)

Instructions:

1. Select Cheeses:
    - Choose a variety of cheeses with different textures and flavors to create a diverse cheese platter. Arrange them on a large serving board or platter.
2. Prepare Crackers:
    - Arrange an assortment of crackers around the cheeses on the serving board. You can use a combination of plain and flavored crackers for variety.
3. Garnish with Fruit:
    - Place clusters of grapes or berries around the cheese and crackers for a pop of color and freshness.
4. Add Nuts:
    - Scatter a handful of nuts, such as almonds, walnuts, or cashews, around the cheese platter for extra crunch and texture.
5. Drizzle with Honey or Preserves (Optional):
    - If desired, drizzle honey or spoon fruit preserves over some of the cheeses for added sweetness and flavor contrast.
6. Garnish with Fresh Herbs:
    - Sprinkle fresh herbs, such as rosemary or thyme leaves, over the cheese platter for a decorative touch and aroma.
7. Serve:
    - Place the cheese and crackers platter in the center of the table and invite guests to help themselves. Provide cheese knives and small plates for serving.

Variations:

- Charcuterie Addition: Enhance your cheese platter by adding cured meats, such as prosciutto, salami, or chorizo, for a charcuterie and cheese board.
- Dried Fruit: Include dried fruits, such as apricots, figs, or cranberries, for additional sweetness and texture.
- Crudités: Serve sliced vegetables, such as carrots, cucumbers, or bell peppers, alongside the cheese and crackers for a refreshing contrast.

This cheese and crackers platter is perfect for entertaining guests at parties, gatherings, or wine nights. Customize it with your favorite cheeses, crackers, and accompaniments for a delicious and elegant appetizer option.

Mini grilled cheese sandwiches

Ingredients:

- Sliced bread (white, whole wheat, or your choice)
- Cheese slices (cheddar, American, Swiss, or any melting cheese of your preference)
- Butter or margarine, softened
- Optional: Additional fillings such as cooked bacon, ham, tomato slices, or caramelized onions

Instructions:

1. Prepare the Bread:
    - Lay out the bread slices on a clean surface. If desired, spread a thin layer of softened butter or margarine on one side of each slice.
2. Assemble the Sandwiches:
    - Place a slice of cheese (and any additional fillings, if using) on the unbuttered side of half of the bread slices. Top with another slice of bread, buttered side facing out, to form sandwiches.
3. Heat Skillet or Griddle:
    - Preheat a skillet or griddle over medium heat. If using a skillet, you may need to add a small amount of butter or oil to prevent sticking.
4. Cook the Sandwiches:
    - Place the assembled sandwiches onto the heated skillet or griddle. Cook for 2-3 minutes on each side, or until the bread is golden brown and crispy, and the cheese is melted.
5. Slice and Serve:
    - Remove the grilled cheese sandwiches from the skillet or griddle and transfer them to a cutting board. Allow them to cool slightly before slicing into smaller pieces or triangles, if desired.
6. Serve Warm:
    - Serve the mini grilled cheese sandwiches warm as a delicious appetizer, snack, or party finger food.

Variations:

- Gourmet Mini Grilled Cheese: Use artisan bread and gourmet cheese varieties, such as brie, gruyere, or fontina, for an elevated twist on classic grilled cheese.
- Vegetarian Mini Grilled Cheese: Add sliced tomatoes, roasted red peppers, or sautéed mushrooms between the cheese slices for a vegetarian-friendly option.
- Sweet and Savory Mini Grilled Cheese: Spread a thin layer of fruit preserves or honey mustard on one slice of bread before assembling the sandwich for a sweet and savory flavor combination.
- Dipping Sauce: Serve mini grilled cheese sandwiches with a side of tomato soup, marinara sauce, or creamy ranch dressing for dipping.

These mini grilled cheese sandwiches are perfect for parties, gatherings, or as a comforting snack any time of day. Customize them with your favorite bread, cheese, and fillings for endless flavor possibilities!

Veggie sticks with dip

Ingredients:

For the Veggie Sticks:

- Carrot sticks
- Celery sticks
- Bell pepper strips (red, yellow, and/or green)
- Cucumber slices
- Cherry tomatoes

For the Dip:

- 1 cup Greek yogurt or sour cream
- 1 tablespoon mayonnaise
- 1 tablespoon lemon juice
- 1 clove garlic, minced
- 1 teaspoon dried dill
- Salt and pepper to taste

Instructions:

1. Prepare the Veggie Sticks:
    - Wash and peel the carrots and cucumber. Cut them into sticks or slices, along with the celery and bell peppers. Arrange the prepared vegetables on a serving platter.
2. Make the Dip:
    - In a small bowl, combine the Greek yogurt or sour cream, mayonnaise, lemon juice, minced garlic, and dried dill. Stir until well combined. Season with salt and pepper to taste.
3. Serve:
    - Transfer the dip to a small serving bowl and place it in the center of the platter with the veggie sticks. Alternatively, you can portion the dip into individual small cups for each guest.
4. Garnish (Optional):
    - Garnish the dip with a sprinkle of dried dill or a few fresh dill sprigs for extra flavor and presentation.
5. Enjoy:
    - Serve the veggie sticks with dip as a healthy and delicious appetizer, snack, or party finger food. Encourage guests to dip the veggies into the creamy dip and enjoy!

Variations:

- Hummus Dip: Substitute the yogurt or sour cream dip with your favorite store-bought or homemade hummus for a creamy and flavorful alternative.
- Ranch Dip: Replace the dill with ranch seasoning mix for a classic ranch-flavored dip that pairs perfectly with crunchy veggies.
- Spicy Dip: Add a pinch of cayenne pepper or a dash of hot sauce to the dip for a spicy kick.

Feel free to customize the veggie sticks and dip with your favorite vegetables and flavors. This healthy and refreshing snack is perfect for parties, gatherings, or as a light appetizer for any occasion!

Mini donuts

Ingredients:

- 1 1/2 cups all-purpose flour
- 1/2 cup granulated sugar
- 1 1/2 teaspoons baking powder
- 1/4 teaspoon baking soda
- 1/2 teaspoon salt
- 1/2 teaspoon ground cinnamon
- 1/4 teaspoon ground nutmeg
- 1/2 cup buttermilk
- 1/4 cup unsalted butter, melted
- 1 large egg
- 1 teaspoon vanilla extract
- Vegetable oil, for frying

For the Glaze:

- 1 cup powdered sugar
- 2-3 tablespoons milk or water
- 1/2 teaspoon vanilla extract

Instructions:

1. Prepare the Batter:
    - In a large bowl, whisk together the flour, sugar, baking powder, baking soda, salt, cinnamon, and nutmeg.
2. Make the Dough:
    - In a separate bowl, whisk together the buttermilk, melted butter, egg, and vanilla extract until well combined. Pour the wet ingredients into the dry ingredients and stir until just combined. Do not overmix; the batter should be slightly lumpy.
3. Fry the Donuts:
    - Heat vegetable oil in a deep fryer or large, heavy-bottomed pot to 350°F (175°C). Use a mini donut maker or a mini donut pan for baking, or shape the dough into small balls for frying.
    - Carefully drop the dough balls into the hot oil, a few at a time, and fry until golden brown, about 2-3 minutes, turning them halfway through cooking. Use a slotted spoon to remove the donuts from the oil and transfer them to a paper towel-lined plate to drain excess oil.
4. Make the Glaze:
    - In a small bowl, whisk together the powdered sugar, milk or water, and vanilla extract until smooth and well combined. Adjust the consistency by adding more milk or powdered sugar as needed.
5. Glaze the Donuts:

- While the donuts are still warm, dip each one into the glaze, coating it completely. Allow any excess glaze to drip off, then place the glazed donuts on a wire rack set over a baking sheet to set.
6. Serve:
    - Serve the mini donuts warm or at room temperature. Enjoy them plain or with your favorite toppings, such as sprinkles, chopped nuts, or chocolate drizzle.

Variations:

- Chocolate Glaze: Add cocoa powder to the glaze mixture for a chocolate-flavored glaze.
- Maple Glaze: Substitute some of the milk or water in the glaze with maple syrup for a delicious maple-flavored glaze.
- Cinnamon Sugar Coating: After frying, toss the warm donuts in a mixture of cinnamon and sugar for a classic cinnamon sugar coating.

These mini donuts are perfect for breakfast, brunch, dessert, or anytime you're craving a sweet treat. Enjoy their deliciousness with friends and family!

Fruit smoothies

Ingredients:

- 1 cup of your favorite fruit (such as berries, banana, mango, pineapple, or a combination)
- 1/2 cup plain Greek yogurt or dairy-free yogurt alternative
- 1/2 cup milk or dairy-free milk alternative (such as almond milk, coconut milk, or soy milk)
- 1-2 tablespoons honey, maple syrup, or agave syrup (optional, for sweetness)
- Ice cubes (optional, for a colder smoothie)

Instructions:

1. Prepare the Fruit:
    - Wash and chop the fruit into small pieces if necessary. If using frozen fruit, there's no need to chop it.
2. Blend Ingredients:
    - In a blender, combine the fruit, Greek yogurt, milk, and sweetener (if using). If you prefer a thicker smoothie, you can add less milk or more yogurt.
3. Blend Until Smooth:
    - Blend the ingredients on high speed until smooth and creamy. If the smoothie is too thick, you can add more milk to reach your desired consistency.
4. Taste and Adjust:
    - Taste the smoothie and adjust the sweetness if needed by adding more honey, maple syrup, or agave syrup.
5. Serve:
    - Pour the fruit smoothie into glasses and serve immediately. You can garnish with additional fruit slices or mint leaves if desired.

Variations:

- Green Smoothie: Add a handful of spinach or kale leaves to the blender for a nutritious green smoothie. You can also add avocado for creaminess.
- Protein Smoothie: Boost the protein content of your smoothie by adding a scoop of protein powder, nut butter, or hemp seeds.
- Tropical Smoothie: Use tropical fruits such as mango, pineapple, and banana for a refreshing tropical smoothie. Add coconut milk for extra tropical flavor.
- Berry Smoothie: Use a combination of berries such as strawberries, blueberries, raspberries, and blackberries for a vibrant and antioxidant-rich smoothie.
- Citrus Smoothie: Add citrus fruits such as oranges, lemons, or limes for a tangy and refreshing citrus smoothie.

Experiment with different fruit combinations and ingredients to create your own delicious fruit smoothie recipes. Enjoy them for breakfast, as a snack, or post-workout refresher!

Rainbow fruit platter

Ingredients:

- Strawberries (red)
- Mandarin oranges or orange slices (orange)
- Pineapple chunks or slices (yellow)
- Kiwi slices (green)
- Blueberries (blue)
- Blackberries or purple grapes (purple)

Optional:

- Raspberries or watermelon cubes (pink)
- Honeydew or green grapes (light green)
- Mango slices (yellow-orange)

Instructions:

1. Prepare the Fruit:
    - Wash all the fruit thoroughly under cold water. Peel, slice, and chop the fruit into bite-sized pieces as needed.
2. Arrange by Color:
    - Begin arranging the fruit on a large serving platter or tray, starting with the strawberries at one end for the red color. Continue arranging the fruit in rows according to their colors of the rainbow.
3. Create the Rainbow:
    - Arrange the mandarin oranges or orange slices next to the strawberries for the orange color, followed by the pineapple for yellow, kiwi for green, blueberries for blue, and blackberries or purple grapes for purple.
4. Optional Additions:
    - If desired, add additional fruit to represent other colors of the rainbow. For example, you can add raspberries or watermelon cubes for pink, honeydew or green grapes for light green, and mango slices for yellow-orange.
5. Garnish (Optional):
    - Garnish the fruit platter with fresh mint leaves or edible flowers for an extra decorative touch.
6. Serve:
    - Serve the rainbow fruit platter immediately as a colorful and nutritious snack or dessert option for parties, gatherings, or special occasions.

Tips

- Keep it Fresh: To keep the fruit fresh and vibrant, assemble the rainbow fruit platter shortly before serving. You can also cover the platter with plastic wrap and store it in the refrigerator until ready to serve.

- Dip or Drizzle: Serve the rainbow fruit platter with a side of yogurt dip, honey, or chocolate sauce for dipping or drizzling over the fruit for added flavor.
- Customize: Feel free to customize the fruit selection based on personal preferences and seasonal availability. Use a variety of fruits to create a visually appealing and delicious rainbow fruit platter.

Enjoy this colorful and refreshing rainbow fruit platter as a healthy and eye-catching addition to any celebration or gathering!

Chicken nuggets

Ingredients:

- 1 lb boneless, skinless chicken breasts or chicken tenders
- 1 cup all-purpose flour
- 2 large eggs
- 1 cup breadcrumbs (plain or seasoned)
- 1 teaspoon garlic powder
- 1 teaspoon onion powder
- 1/2 teaspoon paprika
- Salt and pepper, to taste
- Cooking oil (vegetable oil, canola oil, or olive oil) for frying

Instructions:

1. Prepare the Chicken:
   - Cut the chicken breasts into bite-sized pieces or strips. Pat them dry with paper towels and season with salt and pepper.
2. Set Up Dredging Station:
   - Prepare three shallow bowls or plates. Place the flour in one bowl, beaten eggs in another bowl, and breadcrumbs mixed with garlic powder, onion powder, paprika, salt, and pepper in the third bowl.
3. Dredge the Chicken:
   - Dredge each piece of chicken in the flour, shaking off any excess. Then dip it into the beaten eggs, allowing any excess to drip off. Finally, coat it evenly with the breadcrumb mixture, pressing gently to adhere.
4. Heat the Oil:
   - In a large skillet or frying pan, heat enough cooking oil to cover the bottom of the pan over medium heat until it reaches 350°F (175°C).
5. Fry the Chicken Nuggets:
   - Carefully place the coated chicken pieces into the hot oil in batches, making sure not to overcrowd the pan. Fry for 3-4 minutes on each side, or until golden brown and cooked through. Use a slotted spoon to transfer the cooked chicken nuggets to a paper towel-lined plate to drain excess oil.
6. Serve:
   - Serve the homemade chicken nuggets hot with your favorite dipping sauce, such as ketchup, honey mustard, barbecue sauce, or ranch dressing.

Baking Option:

- If you prefer a healthier alternative to frying, you can bake the chicken nuggets in a preheated oven at 400°F (200°C) for 15-20 minutes, flipping halfway through, until golden and cooked through.

Variations:

- Parmesan Crusted Chicken Nuggets: Add grated Parmesan cheese to the breadcrumb mixture for extra flavor and a crispy crust.
- Spicy Chicken Nuggets: Mix in cayenne pepper or chili powder to the breadcrumb mixture for a spicy kick.
- Gluten-Free Chicken Nuggets: Use gluten-free breadcrumbs or crushed cornflakes for a gluten-free version of chicken nuggets.

These homemade chicken nuggets are sure to be a hit with both kids and adults alike! Enjoy them as a tasty snack, appetizer, or main dish.

Macaroni and cheese bites

Ingredients:

- 1 1/2 cups uncooked elbow macaroni
- 2 tablespoons unsalted butter
- 2 tablespoons all-purpose flour
- 1 cup milk
- 2 cups shredded cheddar cheese
- 1/4 teaspoon garlic powder
- 1/4 teaspoon onion powder
- Salt and pepper, to taste
- 1 large egg
- 1 cup breadcrumbs (plain or seasoned)
- Cooking spray or oil, for greasing

Instructions:

1. Cook the Macaroni:
    - Cook the elbow macaroni according to the package instructions until al dente. Drain and set aside.
2. Make the Cheese Sauce:
    - In a saucepan, melt the butter over medium heat. Stir in the flour and cook for 1-2 minutes to form a roux.
    - Gradually whisk in the milk until smooth and thickened, about 3-4 minutes.
    - Reduce the heat to low and stir in the shredded cheddar cheese until melted and smooth. Season with garlic powder, onion powder, salt, and pepper to taste.
    - Remove the cheese sauce from heat and stir in the cooked macaroni until evenly coated. Let the mixture cool slightly.
3. Form the Bites:
    - Preheat the oven to 375°F (190°C). Grease a mini muffin tin with cooking spray or oil.
    - In a small bowl, lightly beat the egg. Place the breadcrumbs in another small bowl.
    - Using a spoon or cookie scoop, scoop the macaroni and cheese mixture into the greased mini muffin tin, pressing down gently to pack it in.
    - Dip each macaroni and cheese bite into the beaten egg, then coat it evenly with breadcrumbs. Place it back into the mini muffin tin.
4. Bake the Bites:
    - Bake the macaroni and cheese bites in the preheated oven for 20-25 minutes, or until golden brown and crispy.
5. Serve:
    - Allow the macaroni and cheese bites to cool for a few minutes before carefully removing them from the mini muffin tin. Serve warm as a delicious appetizer or snack.

Variations:

- Add-Ins: Customize your macaroni and cheese bites by adding cooked bacon bits, diced ham, chopped broccoli, or diced jalapeños to the mixture before baking.
- Different Cheeses: Experiment with different cheese blends such as mozzarella, Monterey Jack, or Gouda for a unique flavor profile.
- Spices: Enhance the flavor of your macaroni and cheese bites by adding spices such as paprika, cayenne pepper, or dried herbs to the cheese sauce.

These macaroni and cheese bites are perfect for parties, game day snacks, or as a fun appetizer for any occasion. Enjoy their creamy and cheesy goodness in bite-sized form!

Mini fruit pizzas

Ingredients:

For the Cookie Crust:

- 1/2 cup unsalted butter, softened
- 1/2 cup granulated sugar
- 1 large egg
- 1 teaspoon vanilla extract
- 1 1/4 cups all-purpose flour
- 1/2 teaspoon baking powder
- Pinch of salt

For the Cream Cheese Frosting:

- 4 oz cream cheese, softened
- 1/4 cup unsalted butter, softened
- 1 cup powdered sugar
- 1/2 teaspoon vanilla extract

For Topping:

- Assorted fruits such as strawberries, blueberries, kiwi, pineapple, mandarin oranges, grapes, etc., sliced or diced

Instructions:

1. Prepare the Cookie Crust:
    - In a large mixing bowl, cream together the softened butter and granulated sugar until light and fluffy. Beat in the egg and vanilla extract until well combined.
    - In a separate bowl, whisk together the flour, baking powder, and salt. Gradually add the dry ingredients to the wet ingredients, mixing until a soft dough forms.
    - Divide the dough into small portions and roll each portion into a ball. Place the dough balls on a parchment-lined baking sheet, leaving space between each one.
    - Flatten each dough ball with your fingers or the back of a spoon to create mini pizza crusts.
2. Bake the Cookie Crust:
    - Preheat the oven to 350°F (175°C). Bake the cookie crusts for 8-10 minutes, or until lightly golden around the edges. Remove from the oven and let them cool completely on a wire rack.
3. Prepare the Cream Cheese Frosting:
    - In a mixing bowl, beat the softened cream cheese and butter until smooth and creamy. Gradually add the powdered sugar and vanilla extract, beating until the frosting is smooth and well combined. Adjust the sweetness to taste if needed.

4. Assemble the Mini Fruit Pizzas:
   - Once the cookie crusts are cooled, spread a layer of cream cheese frosting over each crust, leaving a small border around the edges.
   - Arrange the sliced or diced fruits on top of the frosting in a decorative pattern. You can mix and match different fruits to create a colorful assortment.
   - Optional: For added sweetness and shine, you can brush a light layer of warmed apricot preserves or honey over the fruit.
5. Serve:
   - Serve the mini fruit pizzas immediately, or chill them in the refrigerator until ready to serve. Enjoy as a delightful dessert or snack!

Variations:

- Chocolate Drizzle: Drizzle melted chocolate over the fruit toppings for an extra indulgent touch.
- Coconut Flakes: Sprinkle toasted coconut flakes over the cream cheese frosting for added texture and flavor.
- Nut Butter Spread: Spread a thin layer of peanut butter or almond butter on the cookie crust before adding the cream cheese frosting and fruit toppings for a nutty twist.

These mini fruit pizzas are perfect for parties, potlucks, or as a fun dessert activity with kids. Get creative with your fruit combinations and enjoy their deliciousness!

Cheese quesadillas

Ingredients:

- 4 large flour tortillas
- 2 cups shredded cheese (such as cheddar, Monterey Jack, or a blend)
- 2 tablespoons unsalted butter or olive oil, divided
- Optional additional fillings:
    - Cooked chicken, beef, or shrimp
    - Sliced bell peppers
    - Diced onions
    - Sliced jalapeños
    - Black beans
    - Corn kernels
    - Salsa
    - Guacamole
    - Sour cream

Instructions:

1. Prepare the Tortillas:
    - Lay out the flour tortillas on a clean surface.
2. Add the Cheese (and Optional Fillings):
    - Sprinkle a generous amount of shredded cheese evenly over half of each tortilla. If desired, add any additional fillings on top of the cheese.
3. Fold the Tortillas:
    - Fold the tortillas in half over the cheese and fillings, creating half-moon shapes.
4. Cook the Quesadillas:
    - In a large skillet or griddle, heat 1 tablespoon of butter or olive oil over medium heat until melted and hot.
    - Place one or two quesadillas in the skillet or griddle, depending on the size of your pan. Cook for 2-3 minutes on each side, or until golden brown and crispy, and the cheese is melted. If needed, press down gently with a spatula to flatten the quesadillas as they cook.
    - Repeat with the remaining quesadillas, adding more butter or oil to the pan as needed.
5. Slice and Serve:
    - Remove the cooked quesadillas from the skillet or griddle and transfer them to a cutting board. Use a sharp knife or pizza cutter to slice each quesadilla into wedges or triangles.
6. Serve with Toppings:
    - Serve the cheese quesadillas hot with your favorite toppings, such as salsa, guacamole, sour cream, or additional cheese.

Variations:

- Protein Additions: Add cooked chicken, beef, or shrimp to the quesadillas for added protein.
- Veggie Quesadillas: Add sliced bell peppers, diced onions, sliced jalapeños, black beans, or corn kernels for a vegetarian-friendly option.
- Cheese Blend: Use a combination of different cheeses for extra flavor. Experiment with Monterey Jack, pepper jack, mozzarella, or queso fresco.

These cheese quesadillas are quick, easy, and versatile, making them perfect for a simple meal or snack any time of day. Enjoy their gooey, cheesy goodness with your favorite toppings!

Pretzel rods dipped in chocolate

Ingredients:

- Pretzel rods
- 8 ounces (about 1 1/2 cups) semisweet chocolate chips or chocolate melting wafers
- Optional toppings:
    - Chopped nuts (such as almonds, pecans, or peanuts)
    - Sprinkles
    - Crushed candy canes
    - Shredded coconut
    - Mini chocolate chips
    - Crushed cookies

Instructions:

1. Prepare the Pretzel Rods:
    - Line a baking sheet with parchment paper or wax paper. Place the pretzel rods on the prepared baking sheet, leaving space between each one.
2. Melt the Chocolate:
    - In a microwave-safe bowl, melt the chocolate chips or chocolate melting wafers in the microwave in 30-second intervals, stirring after each interval, until smooth and fully melted. Alternatively, you can melt the chocolate using a double boiler on the stove.
3. Dip the Pretzel Rods:
    - Holding one pretzel rod at a time, dip it into the melted chocolate, using a spoon or spatula to help coat it evenly. Allow any excess chocolate to drip off.
4. Add Toppings (Optional):
    - If desired, sprinkle the chocolate-coated pretzel rod with your favorite toppings while the chocolate is still wet. You can roll the pretzel rod in chopped nuts, sprinkles, crushed candy canes, shredded coconut, mini chocolate chips, or crushed cookies.
5. Place on Baking Sheet:
    - Place the chocolate-dipped and topped pretzel rod back onto the lined baking sheet, making sure it's not touching any other pretzel rods.
6. Allow to Set:
    - Repeat the dipping and topping process with the remaining pretzel rods. Once all the pretzel rods are coated and topped, allow them to set at room temperature until the chocolate is firm and fully hardened.
7. Serve or Store:
    - Once the chocolate is set, the chocolate-dipped pretzel rods are ready to enjoy! Serve them as a delicious sweet treat or package them in cellophane bags or gift boxes for gifting.
    - Store any leftover chocolate-dipped pretzel rods in an airtight container at room temperature for up to one week.

Variations:

- White Chocolate Coating: Substitute white chocolate chips or white chocolate melting wafers for a different flavor profile.
- Caramel Drizzle: Drizzle melted caramel over the chocolate-coated pretzel rods for an extra decadent touch.
- Holiday Themes: Use themed sprinkles or toppings to match different holidays or occasions, such as red and green sprinkles for Christmas or pastel-colored sprinkles for Easter.

These chocolate-dipped pretzel rods are a delightful combination of sweet and salty, making them perfect for parties, gatherings, or as homemade gifts. Enjoy the crunchy texture and rich chocolate flavor in every bite!

Jello cups

Ingredients:

- 1 (3 oz) package flavored gelatin (such as Jello)
- 1 cup boiling water
- 1 cup cold water
- Optional toppings:
    - Whipped cream
    - Fresh fruit
    - Sprinkles
    - Maraschino cherries
    - Shredded coconut
    - Chocolate shavings

Instructions:

1. Prepare the Gelatin:
    - In a heatproof bowl, dissolve the flavored gelatin powder in 1 cup of boiling water. Stir until the gelatin is completely dissolved.
2. Add Cold Water:
    - Stir in 1 cup of cold water until well combined. This helps cool down the mixture and sets the gelatin.
3. Pour into Cups:
    - Pour the gelatin mixture evenly into individual serving cups or glasses. Use clear cups to showcase the colorful gelatin, if desired.
4. Chill:
    - Place the cups of gelatin in the refrigerator to chill and set completely. This usually takes about 4 hours, but you can speed up the process by placing them in the freezer for 1-2 hours.
5. Add Toppings:
    - Once the gelatin is set, you can add your favorite toppings. Dollop whipped cream on top of each cup and garnish with fresh fruit, sprinkles, maraschino cherries, shredded coconut, chocolate shavings, or any other toppings of your choice.
6. Serve:
    - Serve the jello cups chilled as a refreshing and colorful dessert or snack option.

Variations:

- Layered Jello Cups: Create colorful layered jello cups by allowing each layer of gelatin to set partially before pouring the next layer on top. You can use different flavors and colors for each layer to create a rainbow effect.
- Fruit Jello Cups: Add diced fruit (such as strawberries, oranges, pineapple, or peaches) to the gelatin mixture before chilling for added texture and flavor.

- Creamy Jello Cups: Mix in a dollop of yogurt or canned coconut milk to the gelatin mixture before chilling for a creamier texture.
- Alcoholic Jello Shots: For adult-friendly jello cups, substitute part of the cold water with your favorite alcohol, such as vodka, rum, or tequila.

These jello cups are fun, colorful, and customizable, making them perfect for parties, picnics, or as a sweet treat for any occasion. Enjoy the wiggly, jiggly goodness!

Mini muffins

Ingredients:

- 1 1/2 cups all-purpose flour
- 1/2 cup granulated sugar
- 2 teaspoons baking powder
- 1/2 teaspoon salt
- 1/2 cup milk
- 1/4 cup vegetable oil or melted butter
- 1 large egg
- 1 teaspoon vanilla extract
- Optional add-ins:
    - Chocolate chips
    - Blueberries
    - Chopped nuts
    - Dried fruit
    - Shredded coconut
    - Lemon zest

Instructions:

1. Preheat the Oven:
    - Preheat your oven to 375°F (190°C). Grease or line mini muffin tins with paper liners.
2. Mix Dry Ingredients:
    - In a large bowl, whisk together the flour, sugar, baking powder, and salt until well combined.
3. Combine Wet Ingredients:
    - In another bowl, whisk together the milk, vegetable oil or melted butter, egg, and vanilla extract until smooth.
4. Combine Wet and Dry Ingredients:
    - Pour the wet ingredients into the bowl of dry ingredients. Stir until just combined. Be careful not to overmix; a few lumps are okay.
5. Add Optional Add-Ins:
    - Gently fold in any optional add-ins, such as chocolate chips, blueberries, chopped nuts, dried fruit, shredded coconut, or lemon zest, until evenly distributed throughout the batter.
6. Fill Mini Muffin Tins:
    - Using a spoon or small scoop, fill each mini muffin cup about two-thirds full with the batter.
7. Bake:
    - Bake the mini muffins in the preheated oven for 10-12 minutes, or until a toothpick inserted into the center comes out clean.
8. Cool and Serve:

- Allow the mini muffins to cool in the muffin tins for a few minutes before transferring them to a wire rack to cool completely. Serve warm or at room temperature.

Variations:

- Banana Mini Muffins: Add mashed ripe bananas to the wet ingredients for moist and flavorful banana mini muffins.
- Apple Cinnamon Mini Muffins: Fold diced apples and ground cinnamon into the batter for deliciously spiced mini muffins.
- Zucchini Mini Muffins: Grate zucchini and squeeze out excess moisture before adding it to the batter for moist and tender mini muffins.

These mini muffins are perfect for breakfast, brunch, snacks, or as a sweet treat any time of day. Enjoy their bite-sized goodness!

Fruit salad cups

Ingredients:

- Assorted fresh fruits (such as strawberries, blueberries, grapes, pineapple, kiwi, mango, oranges, apples, and bananas), washed, peeled, and diced
- Optional additional fruits:
    - Raspberries
    - Blackberries
    - Watermelon
    - Honeydew melon
    - Cantaloupe
- Fresh mint leaves, for garnish (optional)
- Lemon juice (optional, to prevent fruit from browning)

Instructions:

1. Prepare the Fruits:
    - Wash all the fruits thoroughly under cold water. Peel and dice them into bite-sized pieces. If using fruits that tend to brown quickly (such as apples and bananas), you can toss them in lemon juice to prevent browning.
2. Mix the Fruit Salad:
    - In a large mixing bowl, combine the diced fruits. Gently toss the fruits together until well mixed.
3. Assemble the Fruit Salad Cups:
    - Divide the mixed fruit salad evenly among individual serving cups or bowls. Use clear cups to showcase the colorful fruits, if desired.
4. Garnish (Optional):
    - Garnish each fruit salad cup with a sprig of fresh mint leaves for an extra pop of color and flavor.
5. Serve:
    - Serve the fruit salad cups immediately as a refreshing and healthy snack or dessert option.

Variations:

- Honey Lime Dressing: Drizzle a mixture of honey and fresh lime juice over the fruit salad for added sweetness and tanginess.
- Coconut Flakes: Sprinkle toasted coconut flakes over the fruit salad for a tropical twist.
- Yogurt Parfait: Layer the fruit salad with vanilla yogurt in serving cups for a creamy and delicious parfait.
- Fruit Skewers: Thread the diced fruits onto skewers for a fun and portable way to enjoy the fruit salad.
- Fruit Salsa: Chop the fruits into smaller pieces and toss them with a squeeze of lime juice and a sprinkle of chopped mint for a refreshing fruit salsa.

Feel free to customize the fruit salad cups with your favorite fruits and toppings. Enjoy the vibrant colors and delicious flavors of this nutritious treat!

S'mores bites

Ingredients:

- 1 cup graham cracker crumbs
- 1/4 cup powdered sugar
- 1/4 cup unsalted butter, melted
- 1 cup semisweet chocolate chips
- 1 cup mini marshmallows

Instructions:

1. Prepare Graham Cracker Base:
    - In a mixing bowl, combine the graham cracker crumbs, powdered sugar, and melted butter. Stir until well combined and the mixture resembles wet sand.
2. Form Crust:
    - Press the graham cracker mixture firmly into the bottom of a greased mini muffin tin. Press down with the back of a spoon or your fingers to create a compact crust in each cavity.
3. Bake Crust:
    - Preheat the oven to 350°F (175°C). Bake the graham cracker crusts for 5 minutes. Remove from the oven and let them cool slightly.
4. Add Chocolate and Marshmallows:
    - Place a few chocolate chips into each graham cracker crust, filling them about halfway. Top the chocolate chips with a few mini marshmallows.
5. Bake Again:
    - Return the muffin tin to the oven and bake for an additional 3-5 minutes, or until the marshmallows are golden brown and puffed up.
6. Cool and Serve:
    - Allow the s'mores bites to cool in the muffin tin for a few minutes before carefully removing them to a wire rack to cool completely.
7. Serve Warm:
    - Serve the s'mores bites warm, allowing the chocolate to melt slightly. Enjoy the gooey, chocolatey goodness!

Variations:

- Nutella Variation: Spread a small spoonful of Nutella on top of the graham cracker crust before adding the chocolate chips and marshmallows for an extra indulgent twist.
- Peanut Butter Add-In: Place a small dollop of peanut butter on top of the graham cracker crust before adding the chocolate chips and marshmallows for a delicious peanut butter s'mores flavor.
- Cookie Crust: Substitute crushed chocolate cookies or Oreos for the graham cracker crumbs to create a cookie crust variation.

- Topping Options: Experiment with different toppings such as caramel sauce, chopped nuts, or sliced strawberries for added flavor and texture.

These s'mores bites are a bite-sized version of the classic campfire treat, perfect for parties, picnics, or anytime you're craving the delicious combination of chocolate, marshmallow, and graham crackers!

Cake batter popcorn

Ingredients:

- 8 cups popped popcorn (about 1/3 cup unpopped kernels)
- 1 cup white chocolate chips or candy melts
- 1/4 cup yellow cake mix
- 2 tablespoons powdered sugar
- Sprinkles (optional)

Instructions:

1. Prepare Popcorn:
    - Pop the popcorn using an air popper or stovetop popcorn maker. Remove any unpopped kernels and place the popped popcorn in a large mixing bowl.
2. Melt White Chocolate:
    - In a microwave-safe bowl, melt the white chocolate chips or candy melts in the microwave in 30-second intervals, stirring after each interval, until smooth and fully melted.
3. Mix Cake Batter:
    - In a small bowl, combine the yellow cake mix and powdered sugar. Mix well to remove any lumps.
4. Coat Popcorn:
    - Pour the melted white chocolate over the popped popcorn in the large mixing bowl. Use a spatula or spoon to gently toss and coat the popcorn evenly with the melted chocolate.
5. Add Cake Batter Mix:
    - Sprinkle the cake batter mix over the coated popcorn. Toss again to evenly distribute the cake batter mix throughout the popcorn.
6. Add Sprinkles (Optional):
    - If desired, add sprinkles to the popcorn mixture and toss gently to incorporate.
7. Let Set:
    - Spread the cake batter popcorn mixture out onto a large baking sheet lined with parchment paper or a silicone mat. Allow it to set at room temperature for about 15-20 minutes, or until the chocolate coating is firm.
8. Serve:
    - Once set, transfer the cake batter popcorn to a serving bowl or individual bags. Enjoy immediately or store in an airtight container for later.

Variations:

- Flavored Cake Mix: Experiment with different flavors of cake mix, such as chocolate, vanilla, or funfetti, to create variations of cake batter popcorn.
- Add-ins: Mix in additional ingredients such as mini chocolate chips, chopped nuts, or dried fruit for added texture and flavor.

- Drizzle: Drizzle melted chocolate or colored candy melts over the cake batter popcorn for extra sweetness and decoration.
- Seasonal Sprinkles: Use themed sprinkles to match different holidays or occasions, such as red and green sprinkles for Christmas or pastel-colored sprinkles for Easter.

This cake batter popcorn is a fun and festive snack that combines the flavors of cake batter and popcorn into a delicious treat. Enjoy its sweet and crunchy goodness at parties, movie nights, or as a special homemade gift!

Sandwich kabobs

Ingredients:

- Sliced bread (white, whole wheat, or your favorite variety)
- Assorted deli meats (such as ham, turkey, roast beef, or chicken)
- Assorted cheeses (such as cheddar, Swiss, provolone, or pepper jack)
- Lettuce leaves
- Cherry tomatoes
- Mini pickles or gherkins
- Olives (black or green)
- Bamboo skewers or toothpicks

Instructions:

1. Prepare Ingredients:
    - Cut the sliced bread into bite-sized squares or rectangles. Fold or roll up the deli meats and slice the cheeses into cubes or squares. Wash and dry the lettuce leaves, cherry tomatoes, mini pickles, and olives.
2. Assemble Kabobs:
    - Thread the ingredients onto bamboo skewers or toothpicks in any combination you like. Start with a piece of bread as the base, followed by folded or rolled-up deli meat, cheese, lettuce leaf, cherry tomato, mini pickle, and olive. Repeat until the skewer is filled, leaving a small space at the top for easy handling.
3. Serve:
    - Arrange the sandwich kabobs on a serving platter or stand for a fun and creative presentation. Serve them as appetizers, snacks, or party finger foods.
4. Variations:
    - Vegetarian Option: Substitute deli meats with sliced tofu, grilled vegetables (such as zucchini, bell peppers, or mushrooms), or marinated tofu or tempeh.
    - Dipping Sauces: Serve the sandwich kabobs with dipping sauces such as ranch dressing, honey mustard, barbecue sauce, or hummus for added flavor.
    - Customize Fillings: Customize the fillings according to your preferences and dietary restrictions. Add sliced cucumbers, bell peppers, or avocado for extra crunch and flavor.
    - Kids' Favorite: Let kids assemble their own sandwich kabobs by providing a variety of ingredients and letting them create their own combinations. It's a fun and interactive way to involve them in meal preparation.

These sandwich kabobs are not only delicious and versatile but also make a visually appealing add tion to any party or gathering. Enjoy the convenience of a sandwich in a bite-sized and portable form!

Mini fruit tarts

Ingredients:

For the Tart Crust:

- 1 1/4 cups all-purpose flour
- 1/4 cup granulated sugar
- 1/2 cup unsalted butter, cold and cut into small pieces
- 1 large egg yolk
- 1-2 tablespoons ice water, if needed

For the Pastry Cream:

- 1 cup whole milk
- 1/4 cup granulated sugar
- 2 large egg yolks
- 2 tablespoons cornstarch
- 1 teaspoon vanilla extract

For Assembly:

- Assorted fresh fruits (such as strawberries, blueberries, raspberries, kiwi, and mandarin oranges), washed and sliced
- Apricot jam or preserves, for glazing (optional)
- Fresh mint leaves, for garnish (optional)

Instructions:

1. Prepare the Tart Crust:
    - In a food processor, pulse together the flour and sugar. Add the cold butter pieces and pulse until the mixture resembles coarse crumbs.
    - Add the egg yolk and pulse until the dough comes together. If the dough is too dry, add 1-2 tablespoons of ice water, one tablespoon at a time, until it forms a ball.
    - Flatten the dough into a disk, wrap it in plastic wrap, and refrigerate for at least 30 minutes.
2. Roll Out and Cut the Dough:
    - Preheat the oven to 375°F (190°C). On a lightly floured surface, roll out the chilled dough to about 1/8 inch thickness. Using a round cookie cutter or glass, cut out circles slightly larger than the wells of your mini muffin tin.
    - Press the dough circles into the wells of the mini muffin tin, shaping them into mini tart shells. Prick the bottoms of the tart shells with a fork to prevent them from puffing up during baking.
3. Bake the Tart Shells:

- Bake the tart shells in the preheated oven for 10-12 minutes, or until lightly golden brown. Remove from the oven and let them cool completely in the tin.
4. Prepare the Pastry Cream:
    - In a saucepan, heat the milk over medium heat until it just begins to simmer. In a separate bowl, whisk together the sugar, egg yolks, and cornstarch until smooth.
    - Slowly pour the hot milk into the egg mixture, whisking constantly to prevent curdling. Return the mixture to the saucepan and cook over medium heat, stirring constantly, until thickened.
    - Remove from heat and stir in the vanilla extract. Transfer the pastry cream to a bowl and cover it with plastic wrap, pressing the plastic wrap directly onto the surface to prevent a skin from forming. Refrigerate until completely chilled.
5. Assemble the Mini Fruit Tarts:
    - Once the tart shells and pastry cream are completely cooled, spoon a small amount of pastry cream into each tart shell, filling them about halfway.
    - Arrange the sliced fresh fruits on top of the pastry cream in a decorative pattern. If desired, warm apricot jam or preserves in a small saucepan over low heat and brush it lightly over the fruit to glaze.
    - Garnish each mini fruit tart with a fresh mint leaf, if desired.
6. Serve:
    - Serve the mini fruit tarts immediately, or refrigerate them until ready to serve. Enjoy these delightful bite-sized treats!

Variations:

- Chocolate Ganache: Instead of pastry cream, fill the tart shells with chocolate ganache for a rich and indulgent twist.
- Lemon Curd: Substitute lemon curd for the pastry cream for a tangy and citrusy flavor.
- Almond Frangipane: Fill the tart shells with almond frangipane (almond cream) and top with fresh fruits for an elegant and nutty flavor profile.

These mini fruit tarts are not only beautiful to look at but also bursting with fresh fruit flavors and creamy pastry cream. They make a perfect dessert for any occasion or celebration!

Chocolate fondue with dippers

Ingredients:

For the Chocolate Fondue:

- 8 ounces (about 1 1/2 cups) semisweet chocolate, chopped
- 1/2 cup heavy cream
- 1 tablespoon unsalted butter
- 1 teaspoon vanilla extract
- Pinch of salt

For Dipping:

- Fresh fruit (such as strawberries, banana slices, pineapple chunks, apple slices, or grapes)
- Marshmallows
- Pretzel rods or sticks
- Pound cake or angel food cake, cut into cubes
- Cookies (such as shortbread, biscotti, or graham crackers)
- Dried fruit (such as apricots, cherries, or figs)
- Nuts (such as almonds, cashews, or pecans)

Instructions:

1. Prepare the Chocolate Fondue:
    - In a heatproof bowl set over a pot of simmering water (double boiler), combine the chopped semisweet chocolate, heavy cream, butter, vanilla extract, and salt. Stir continuously until the chocolate is melted and the mixture is smooth and well combined. Alternatively, you can melt the chocolate and cream together in the microwave in 30-second intervals, stirring in between until smooth.
2. Keep Warm:
    - Transfer the melted chocolate fondue to a fondue pot or a heatproof serving bowl. Keep the fondue warm over a low flame or use a fondue pot with a tea light candle or burner to maintain a gentle heat.
3. Prepare Dippers:
    - Wash and prepare the fresh fruit by slicing or cutting them into bite-sized pieces. Arrange the fruit, marshmallows, pretzel rods, cake cubes, cookies, dried fruit, and nuts on a serving platter or in individual bowls.
4. Dip and Enjoy:
    - Spear your choice of dippers onto fondue forks or skewers and dip them into the warm chocolate fondue. Swirl them around to coat evenly and enjoy the delicious combination of melted chocolate and your favorite dippers.
5. Variations:

- White Chocolate Fondue: Substitute white chocolate for a sweeter and creamier fondue option.
- Flavored Fondue: Add a splash of liqueur, such as Grand Marnier, Kahlua, or Amaretto, to the chocolate fondue for a flavorful twist.
- Spiced Fondue: Stir in a pinch of cinnamon, nutmeg, or chili powder for a hint of spice in the chocolate fondue.
- Decorate: Sprinkle crushed nuts, shredded coconut, or colorful sprinkles over the dipped items for added texture and visual appeal.

Chocolate fondue with dippers is a delightful and interactive dessert that's perfect for parties, gatherings, or romantic evenings at home. Enjoy the creamy, decadent chocolate paired with a variety of delicious dippers for a memorable sweet treat!

Mini bagel pizzas

Ingredients:

- Mini bagels, sliced in half
- Pizza sauce or marinara sauce
- Shredded mozzarella cheese
- Assorted toppings:
    - Pepperoni slices
    - Sliced bell peppers
    - Sliced mushrooms
    - Diced onions
    - Cooked sausage crumbles
    - Black olives, sliced
    - Pineapple tidbits
    - Cherry tomatoes, sliced
    - Fresh basil leaves, torn
- Olive oil (optional)
- Italian seasoning (optional)
- Red pepper flakes (optional)

Instructions:

1. Preheat the Oven:
    - Preheat your oven to 375°F (190°C) and line a baking sheet with parchment paper or aluminum foil.
2. Prepare Bagel Halves:
    - Place the mini bagel halves on the prepared baking sheet, cut side up.
3. Add Sauce:
    - Spread a spoonful of pizza sauce or marinara sauce onto each bagel half, covering the surface evenly.
4. Add Cheese and Toppings:
    - Sprinkle shredded mozzarella cheese generously over the sauce on each bagel half.
    - Add your favorite toppings, such as pepperoni slices, bell peppers, mushrooms, onions, sausage crumbles, black olives, pineapple tidbits, cherry tomatoes, or fresh basil leaves.
5. Optional Seasonings:
    - Drizzle a little olive oil over the toppings for added flavor and shine, if desired.
    - Sprinkle Italian seasoning and red pepper flakes over the pizzas for extra seasoning and heat, if desired.
6. Bake:
    - Place the baking sheet with the assembled mini bagel pizzas in the preheated oven.

- Bake for 10-12 minutes, or until the cheese is melted and bubbly, and the bagel edges are golden brown.
7. Serve:
    - Remove the mini bagel pizzas from the oven and let them cool for a few minutes before serving.
    - Serve the pizzas warm and enjoy their delicious flavors!

Variations:

- Vegetarian Option: Make vegetarian mini bagel pizzas by omitting the meat toppings and loading up on vegetables such as bell peppers, mushrooms, onions, olives, and tomatoes.
- Customize Toppings: Customize the toppings according to your preferences or dietary restrictions. You can also let each person assemble their own mini bagel pizzas with their favorite toppings.
- Cheese Blend: Experiment with different cheese blends such as mozzarella, cheddar, Parmesan, or provolone for a unique flavor profile.
- Breakfast Pizzas: Turn mini bagel pizzas into a breakfast treat by topping them with scrambled eggs, cooked bacon or sausage, and shredded cheese.

These mini bagel pizzas are perfect for quick meals, snacks, or entertaining guests. They're easy to customize and always a hit with both kids and adults alike!

Rainbow popcorn

Ingredients:

- 1/2 cup popcorn kernels
- 2 tablespoons vegetable oil
- 1 cup granulated sugar
- 1/4 cup water
- Food coloring (red, orange, yellow, green, blue, purple)
- Salt (optional)

Instructions:

1. Pop the Popcorn:
    - In a large pot, heat the vegetable oil over medium heat. Add the popcorn kernels and cover the pot with a lid. Shake the pot occasionally to prevent burning. Once the popping slows down, remove the pot from the heat and let it sit for a minute to allow any remaining kernels to pop. Transfer the popcorn to a large mixing bowl and set aside.
2. Prepare the Rainbow Syrup:
    - In a small saucepan, combine the granulated sugar and water. Heat the mixture over medium heat, stirring constantly, until the sugar is completely dissolved and the mixture comes to a boil. Remove the saucepan from the heat.
3. Color the Syrup:
    - Divide the sugar syrup evenly into six small bowls or cups. Add a few drops of food coloring to each bowl to create red, orange, yellow, green, blue, and purple syrups. Stir well until the color is evenly distributed and you achieve the desired intensity.
4. Coat the Popcorn:
    - Working quickly, drizzle each color of syrup over the popped popcorn in the mixing bowl. Use a spoon or spatula to gently toss and coat the popcorn evenly with the colored syrups. Be careful not to crush the popcorn kernels.
5. Let the Popcorn Set:
    - Spread the colored popcorn out onto a large baking sheet lined with parchment paper or a silicone mat. Allow the popcorn to cool and the syrup to set for about 10-15 minutes.
6. Serve or Store:
    - Once the rainbow popcorn has set, you can serve it immediately or store it in an airtight container for later. Enjoy the colorful and sweet treat!

Optional:

- If desired, sprinkle a little salt over the popcorn before adding the colored syrups for a sweet and salty flavor contrast.

Variations:

- Glitter Popcorn: Add edible glitter or shimmer dust to the colored syrups for a sparkling effect.
- Flavored Syrups: Experiment with flavored syrups by adding extracts or flavorings such as vanilla, strawberry, orange, lemon, mint, or almond to the sugar syrup before coloring.
- Mix-ins: Toss in some colorful candy sprinkles or mini marshmallows with the popcorn for added texture and fun.

This rainbow popcorn is a colorful and festive snack that's perfect for parties, movie nights, or any occasion that calls for a little extra cheer!

Yogurt parfait cups

Ingredients:

- 2 cups Greek yogurt (plain or flavored)
- 1 cup granola
- 1 cup mixed fresh fruit (such as berries, sliced bananas, diced mangoes, or kiwi)
- 1/4 cup honey or maple syrup (optional)
- Fresh mint leaves, for garnish (optional)

Instructions:

1. Layer Yogurt and Granola:
    - Begin by spooning a layer of Greek yogurt into the bottom of each parfait cup or glass, filling it about one-third full. Use plain yogurt for a tangier flavor or flavored yogurt for added sweetness.
2. Add Granola:
    - Sprinkle a layer of granola over the yogurt in each cup. You can use your favorite store-bought granola or make homemade granola for a customized touch.
3. Layer Fresh Fruit:
    - Arrange a layer of mixed fresh fruit on top of the granola in each cup. Use a variety of colorful fruits for a visually appealing presentation and a burst of flavor.
4. Repeat Layers:
    - Repeat the layers of yogurt, granola, and fresh fruit until the parfait cups are filled to the top, finishing with a layer of fresh fruit on top.
5. Drizzle with Honey or Maple Syrup (Optional):
    - For added sweetness, drizzle a little honey or maple syrup over the top layer of fresh fruit in each parfait cup.
6. Garnish (Optional):
    - Garnish each yogurt parfait cup with a fresh mint leaf for a decorative touch and a hint of freshness.
7. Serve:
    - Serve the yogurt parfait cups immediately as a nutritious breakfast, satisfying snack, or refreshing dessert option.

Variations:

- Nutty Crunch: Add a sprinkling of chopped nuts or seeds (such as almonds, walnuts, pecans, or pumpkin seeds) between the layers for added crunch and protein.
- Chocolate Indulgence: Layer chocolate granola or chocolate chips between the yogurt and fruit layers for a decadent twist.
- Creamy Texture: Mix a little honey or maple syrup into the Greek yogurt before layering for added sweetness and a smoother texture.
- Frozen Treat: Freeze the yogurt parfait cups for a few hours to create a refreshing frozen yogurt parfait that's perfect for hot summer days.

Yogurt parfait cups are not only delicious and satisfying but also versatile and customizable to suit your taste preferences. Enjoy these nutritious and flavorful treats any time of day!

Mini chicken sliders

Ingredients:

For the Chicken Patties:

- 1 pound ground chicken
- 1/4 cup breadcrumbs
- 1/4 cup grated Parmesan cheese
- 1 large egg
- 2 cloves garlic, minced
- 1 teaspoon dried oregano
- 1 teaspoon dried basil
- Salt and pepper to taste
- Olive oil for cooking

For Assembly:

- Mini slider buns or dinner rolls
- Lettuce leaves
- Sliced tomatoes
- Sliced red onions
- Sliced pickles
- Mayonnaise
- Mustard
- Ketchup
- Optional: cheese slices (such as cheddar or Swiss)

Instructions:

1. Prepare the Chicken Patties:
    - In a large mixing bowl, combine the ground chicken, breadcrumbs, grated Parmesan cheese, egg, minced garlic, dried oregano, dried basil, salt, and pepper. Mix until well combined.
    - Divide the mixture into small portions and shape them into mini chicken patties, slightly larger than the size of your slider buns.
2. Cook the Chicken Patties:
    - Heat a drizzle of olive oil in a large skillet over medium heat. Add the chicken patties to the skillet and cook for 3-4 minutes on each side, or until golden brown and cooked through. Make sure the internal temperature of the patties reaches 165°F (74°C).
3. Assemble the Sliders:
    - Slice the slider buns or dinner rolls in half horizontally. Place a lettuce leaf on the bottom half of each bun.
    - Top the lettuce with a cooked chicken patty.

- Add sliced tomatoes, red onions, pickles, and any other desired toppings on top of the chicken patties.
    - Spread mayonnaise, mustard, and ketchup on the top half of each bun.
    - Optionally, add a slice of cheese on top of the chicken patties before assembling the sliders.
4. Serve:
    - Place the top half of each bun over the toppings to complete the sliders.
    - Secure each slider with a toothpick if necessary.
    - Arrange the mini chicken sliders on a serving platter and serve immediately.

Variations:

- Spicy Chicken Sliders: Add diced jalapeños or a dash of hot sauce to the chicken mixture for a spicy kick.
- BBQ Chicken Sliders: Brush the chicken patties with barbecue sauce during the last few minutes of cooking for a tangy and flavorful twist.
- Asian-Inspired Sliders: Season the chicken patties with soy sauce, ginger, and garlic powder, and top them with Asian slaw and Sriracha mayo.
- Buffalo Chicken Sliders: Toss the cooked chicken patties in buffalo sauce before assembling the sliders, and serve with blue cheese dressing and celery sticks.

These mini chicken sliders are perfect for parties, game days, or any casual gathering. They're easy to customize with your favorite toppings and sauces for a delicious handheld meal!

Candy apples

Ingredients:

- 6-8 medium-sized apples (Granny Smith or Fuji)
- 2 cups granulated sugar
- 1/2 cup light corn syrup
- 1/2 cup water
- Red food coloring (optional)
- 1 teaspoon vanilla extract (optional)
- Candy thermometer
- Wooden sticks or lollipop sticks

Instructions:

1. Prepare the Apples:
    - Wash and dry the apples thoroughly. Remove any stems and insert wooden sticks or lollipop sticks into the stem end of each apple. Set aside on a parchment-lined baking sheet.
2. Make the Candy Coating:
    - In a medium saucepan, combine the granulated sugar, light corn syrup, and water over medium-high heat. Stir until the sugar is dissolved.
3. Cook the Candy Mixture:
    - Once the sugar is dissolved, insert a candy thermometer into the saucepan. Bring the mixture to a boil without stirring. Cook until the temperature reaches 300°F (149°C), also known as the hard crack stage. This will take about 20-25 minutes.
4. Add Food Coloring and Flavoring (Optional):
    - Once the candy mixture reaches 300°F (149°C), remove it from the heat. Carefully add a few drops of red food coloring and vanilla extract, if desired, and stir until evenly incorporated. Be cautious as the mixture may bubble up.
5. Coat the Apples:
    - Working quickly, carefully dip each apple into the hot candy mixture, tilting the saucepan to coat the apple evenly. Allow any excess candy coating to drip back into the saucepan.
6. Let the Candy Apples Cool:
    - Place the coated apples onto the parchment-lined baking sheet and allow them to cool at room temperature until the candy coating hardens, about 20-30 minutes.
7. Serve or Store:
    - Once the candy coating has hardened, your candy apples are ready to enjoy! Serve them immediately, or store them in an airtight container in the refrigerator for up to 2-3 days.

Tips:

- Safety First: Be extremely careful when working with hot sugar syrup as it can cause severe burns. Keep children away from the cooking area.
- Use a Candy Thermometer: It's essential to use a candy thermometer to ensure the candy coating reaches the correct temperature. This ensures that the coating sets properly and gives the candy apples their signature crunchy texture.
- Work Quickly: The candy coating will harden fast, so work quickly to coat the apples once the mixture reaches the desired temperature.
- Variations: Get creative with your candy apples by rolling them in chopped nuts, sprinkles, or crushed candies after dipping them in the candy coating for added texture and flavor.

Enjoy making and indulging in these classic treats, perfect for autumn festivals, Halloween, or any sweet occasion!

Mini corn dogs

Ingredients:

- 1 package (about 8-10) hot dogs or cocktail sausages
- 1 cup yellow cornmeal
- 1 cup all-purpose flour
- 1/4 cup granulated sugar
- 1 tablespoon baking powder
- 1/2 teaspoon salt
- 1 large egg
- 1 cup milk
- Vegetable oil, for frying
- Wooden skewers or toothpicks

Instructions:

1. Prepare the Hot Dogs:
    - If using hot dogs, slice them into bite-sized pieces, about 2-3 inches long. If using cocktail sausages, you can use them as is.
2. Insert Skewers or Toothpicks:
    - Insert wooden skewers or toothpicks into one end of each hot dog or cocktail sausage, leaving enough space to hold onto the stick.
3. Make the Batter:
    - In a large mixing bowl, whisk together the yellow cornmeal, all-purpose flour, granulated sugar, baking powder, and salt until well combined.
    - In a separate bowl, beat the egg and milk together until smooth. Pour the wet ingredients into the dry ingredients and stir until a smooth batter forms.
4. Heat the Oil:
    - In a deep fryer or large pot, heat vegetable oil to 350°F (175°C). Make sure there is enough oil to fully submerge the mini corn dogs.
5. Coat the Hot Dogs:
    - Dip each hot dog or cocktail sausage into the batter, ensuring it is evenly coated on all sides.
6. Fry the Mini Corn Dogs:
    - Carefully place the coated hot dogs into the hot oil, a few at a time, making sure not to overcrowd the fryer. Fry for 2-3 minutes, or until golden brown and cooked through, turning occasionally for even browning.
7. Drain and Serve:
    - Use a slotted spoon or tongs to remove the mini corn dogs from the oil and transfer them to a plate lined with paper towels to drain excess oil.
    - Repeat the frying process with the remaining hot dogs until all are cooked.
    - Serve the mini corn dogs warm with your favorite dipping sauces, such as ketchup, mustard, or honey mustard.

Tips:

- Skewer Safety: Make sure to warn guests about the wooden skewers or toothpicks before serving, especially if children will be eating them.
- Batter Consistency: If the batter is too thick, you can thin it out with a little more milk. If it's too thin, add a bit more flour until you reach the desired consistency.
- Variations: Experiment with different types of sausages or hot dogs for variety. You can also add spices like paprika or cayenne pepper to the batter for extra flavor.

These mini corn dogs are perfect for parties, game days, or as a fun snack for the whole family. Enjoy their crispy exterior and juicy interior with your favorite dipping sauces!

Rainbow grilled cheese sandwiches

Ingredients:

- Slices of bread (white, whole wheat, or your favorite variety)
- Butter or margarine, softened
- Assorted natural food coloring (red, orange, yellow, green, blue, purple)
- Sliced cheese (cheddar, mozzarella, or your favorite melting cheese)

Instructions:

1. Prepare the Bread:
    - Lay out the slices of bread on a clean surface.
2. Color the Butter:
    - Divide the softened butter into six small bowls.
    - Add a few drops of natural food coloring to each bowl, using a different color for each bowl. Mix well until the butter is evenly colored.
3. Spread the Butter:
    - Spread a different color of butter onto one side of each slice of bread. Make sure to cover the entire surface evenly with butter.
4. Assemble the Sandwiches:
    - Place a slice of cheese between two slices of bread, with the buttered sides facing outward.
5. Cook the Sandwiches:
    - Heat a skillet or griddle over medium heat. Place the assembled sandwiches onto the skillet or griddle.
    - Cook the sandwiches for 2-3 minutes on each side, or until the bread is golden brown and the cheese is melted.
    - If desired, press down gently on the sandwiches with a spatula while cooking to help them cook evenly and encourage the cheese to melt.
6. Serve:
    - Once the sandwiches are cooked to your liking, remove them from the skillet or griddle.
    - Allow them to cool for a minute or two before slicing.
    - Serve the rainbow grilled cheese sandwiches warm and enjoy their colorful and delicious goodness!

Tips:

- Natural Food Coloring: Use natural food coloring made from fruits and vegetables for vibrant colors without artificial additives.
- Variations: Experiment with different types of cheese or add extra ingredients like sliced tomatoes, spinach leaves, or cooked bacon for added flavor and texture.
- Presentation: For extra fun, cut the sandwiches into different shapes using cookie cutters before serving.

These rainbow grilled cheese sandwiches are not only visually appealing but also tasty and fun to make. Enjoy them as a delightful snack or a colorful addition to any meal!

Marshmallow cereal bars

Ingredients:

- 6 cups crispy rice cereal (such as Rice Krispies)
- 4 cups miniature marshmallows
- 3 tablespoons unsalted butter
- Cooking spray or extra butter, for greasing

Optional Add-Ins:

- 1/2 cup chocolate chips
- 1/2 cup chopped nuts (such as almonds or pecans)
- 1/2 cup dried fruit (such as cranberries or raisins)

Instructions:

1. Prepare the Pan:
    - Grease a 9x13-inch baking dish with cooking spray or butter. Set aside.
2. Melt the Marshmallows and Butter:
    - In a large saucepan, melt the butter over medium-low heat.
    - Add the miniature marshmallows to the saucepan, stirring constantly until they are completely melted and smooth. Remove the saucepan from the heat.
3. Mix in the Cereal and Optional Add-Ins:
    - Pour the crispy rice cereal into the saucepan with the melted marshmallows.
    - If desired, add any optional add-ins such as chocolate chips, chopped nuts, or dried fruit. Stir until the cereal and add-ins are evenly coated with the marshmallow mixture.
4. Press into the Pan:
    - Transfer the marshmallow cereal mixture into the greased baking dish.
    - Using a spatula or greased hands, press the mixture firmly and evenly into the pan to create an even layer.
5. Let Cool and Set:
    - Allow the marshmallow cereal bars to cool and set at room temperature for at least 30 minutes, or until firm.
6. Cut and Serve:
    - Once the bars are completely cooled and set, use a sharp knife to cut them into squares or rectangles.
    - Serve the marshmallow cereal bars immediately, or store them in an airtight container at room temperature for up to several days.

Tips:

- Variations: Feel free to customize the marshmallow cereal bars by adding your favorite mix-ins such as chocolate chips, nuts, dried fruit, or even sprinkles.
- Butter Substitute: You can use margarine or coconut oil instead of butter if preferred.

- Storage: Store any leftover marshmallow cereal bars in an airtight container at room temperature for optimal freshness. If the weather is warm, you may want to store them in the refrigerator to prevent them from becoming too soft.

These marshmallow cereal bars are a classic and delicious treat that's perfect for snacking, dessert, or even breakfast on the go! Enjoy their sweet and crispy goodness anytime.

Mini pancakes

Ingredients:

- 1 cup all-purpose flour
- 2 tablespoons granulated sugar
- 1 teaspoon baking powder
- 1/2 teaspoon baking soda
- 1/4 teaspoon salt
- 1 cup buttermilk (or substitute with milk)
- 1 large egg
- 2 tablespoons unsalted butter, melted
- 1 teaspoon vanilla extract
- Cooking spray or additional butter, for greasing

Optional Toppings:

- Maple syrup
- Fresh berries (such as blueberries, strawberries, or raspberries)
- Sliced bananas
- Chocolate chips
- Whipped cream
- Powdered sugar

Instructions:

1. Preheat the Griddle or Pan:
    - Preheat a non-stick griddle or large skillet over medium heat. If using a skillet, lightly grease it with cooking spray or butter.
2. Prepare the Batter:
    - In a large mixing bowl, whisk together the flour, sugar, baking powder, baking soda, and salt until well combined.
3. Mix Wet Ingredients:
    - In a separate bowl, whisk together the buttermilk, egg, melted butter, and vanilla extract until smooth.
4. Combine Wet and Dry Ingredients:
    - Pour the wet ingredients into the dry ingredients and gently stir until just combined. Be careful not to overmix; it's okay if there are a few lumps in the batter.
5. Cook the Mini Pancakes:
    - Once the griddle or skillet is hot, use a tablespoon or small cookie scoop to drop small dollops of batter onto the cooking surface. Leave some space between each pancake as they will spread slightly.
6. Flip When Bubbles Form:

- Cook the mini pancakes for 1-2 minutes, or until bubbles form on the surface and the edges start to look set.
7. Flip and Cook Until Golden:
    - Carefully flip each pancake with a spatula and cook for an additional 1-2 minutes on the other side, or until golden brown and cooked through.
8. Repeat and Keep Warm:
    - Continue cooking the remaining batter in batches, greasing the griddle or skillet as needed between batches. You can keep the cooked mini pancakes warm in a low oven while you finish cooking the rest.
9. Serve and Enjoy:
    - Serve the mini pancakes warm with your favorite toppings, such as maple syrup, fresh berries, sliced bananas, chocolate chips, whipped cream, or powdered sugar.

Tips:

- Size Consistency: For uniform mini pancakes, use a tablespoon or small cookie scoop to measure out the batter for each pancake.
- Customization: Get creative with your toppings! Experiment with different fruits, spreads, or syrups to customize your mini pancakes to your liking.
- Make-Ahead: You can make the batter ahead of time and store it covered in the refrigerator for up to 24 hours. Just give it a quick stir before using.

These mini pancakes are perfect for breakfast, brunch, or even as a sweet snack. Enjoy their fluffy texture and delicious flavor with your favorite toppings!

Cucumber sandwiches

Ingredients:

- 1 large cucumber, thinly sliced
- 8 slices of bread (white, whole wheat, or your choice)
- 4 ounces (about 115g) cream cheese, softened
- 2 tablespoons mayonnaise
- 1 tablespoon chopped fresh dill (optional)
- Salt and pepper to taste
- Butter, softened (optional)

Instructions:

1. Prepare the Cucumber:
    - Wash the cucumber thoroughly and pat it dry with paper towels. Using a sharp knife or a mandoline slicer, thinly slice the cucumber into rounds. Set aside.
2. Make the Cream Cheese Spread:
    - In a mixing bowl, combine the softened cream cheese, mayonnaise, and chopped fresh dill (if using). Mix well until smooth and creamy. Season with salt and pepper to taste.
3. Assemble the Sandwiches:
    - Lay out the slices of bread on a clean surface. If desired, lightly butter one side of each slice of bread for added flavor.
    - Spread a generous layer of the cream cheese mixture onto one side of each slice of bread.
4. Add the Cucumber Slices:
    - Arrange the thinly sliced cucumber rounds evenly on top of the cream cheese mixture, covering the entire surface of half of the bread slices.
5. Complete the Sandwiches:
    - Place the remaining slices of bread, cream cheese side down, on top of the cucumber slices to form sandwiches.
6. Trim the Crusts (Optional):
    - If desired, use a sharp knife to trim the crusts off the sandwiches for a more refined presentation.
7. Slice and Serve:
    - Cut the sandwiches into halves or quarters, depending on your preference.
    - Serve the cucumber sandwiches immediately as a light and refreshing snack, appetizer, or part of a tea party spread.

Variations:

- Herb Butter: Instead of plain butter, you can use herb butter for added flavor. Simply mix softened butter with chopped fresh herbs such as dill, chives, parsley, or mint before spreading it onto the bread slices.

- Additional Fillings: Enhance the flavor and texture of your cucumber sandwiches by adding additional fillings such as thinly sliced radishes, watercress, alfalfa sprouts, or smoked salmon.
- Bread Options: Experiment with different types of bread for your cucumber sandwiches, such as whole grain, rye, pumpernickel, or crustless sandwich bread for an elegant touch.

These cucumber sandwiches are a classic and elegant choice for a light lunch, afternoon tea, or any occasion where you want to impress with a simple yet sophisticated dish. Enjoy their crisp, cool flavor and creamy texture!

Mini spring rolls

Ingredients:

- 1 package of spring roll wrappers (also known as rice paper wrappers)
- 1 cup cooked vermicelli rice noodles
- 1 cup shredded lettuce or cabbage
- 1 cup shredded carrots
- 1 cup thinly sliced cucumber
- 1/2 cup fresh herbs (such as cilantro, mint, and Thai basil)
- Cooked protein of your choice (shredded chicken, cooked shrimp, tofu, or shredded pork), optional
- Warm water, for soaking the rice paper wrappers
- Dipping sauce of your choice (such as sweet chili sauce, peanut sauce, or soy sauce)

Instructions:

1. Prepare the Ingredients:
   - Cook the vermicelli rice noodles according to the package instructions, then drain and set aside to cool.
   - Prepare all the vegetables and herbs by washing, shredding, and slicing them into thin strips. If using cooked protein, shred or slice it into small pieces.
2. Soften the Rice Paper Wrappers:
   - Fill a shallow dish or large bowl with warm water.
   - Dip one rice paper wrapper into the warm water and rotate it gently until it softens, about 15-20 seconds. Be careful not to over-soak, as the wrapper will become too fragile to handle.
3. Assemble the Mini Spring Rolls:
   - Lay the softened rice paper wrapper flat on a clean work surface.
   - Place a small amount of cooked vermicelli rice noodles in the center of the wrapper, followed by a layer of shredded lettuce or cabbage, shredded carrots, sliced cucumber, fresh herbs, and any cooked protein if using.
4. Roll the Spring Rolls:
   - Fold the bottom edge of the rice paper wrapper over the filling, then fold in the sides, and roll it up tightly into a cylinder, similar to rolling a burrito.
   - Repeat the process with the remaining rice paper wrappers and filling ingredients.
5. Serve the Mini Spring Rolls:
   - Arrange the mini spring rolls on a serving platter.
   - Serve immediately with your choice of dipping sauce on the side.

Tips:

- Keep Ingredients Dry: Make sure the filling ingredients are dry before assembling the spring rolls to prevent the wrappers from becoming soggy.

- Customize Fillings: Feel free to customize the fillings based on your preferences and dietary restrictions. You can add or omit ingredients according to taste and availability.
- Serve Fresh: Mini spring rolls are best served fresh to maintain their crispness If preparing in advance, cover them with a damp paper towel or plastic wrap to prevent drying out.

These mini spring rolls are perfect for serving as appetizers, snacks, or light meals. Enjoy their fresh and vibrant flavors, and don't forget to dip them in your favorite sauce for an extra burst of flavor!

Brownie bites

Ingredients:

- 1/2 cup (1 stick) unsalted butter
- 1 cup granulated sugar
- 2 large eggs
- 1 teaspoon vanilla extract
- 1/3 cup unsweetened cocoa powder
- 1/2 cup all-purpose flour
- 1/4 teaspoon salt
- 1/4 teaspoon baking powder
- Optional: 1/2 cup chocolate chips, nuts, or other mix-ins

Instructions:

1. Preheat the Oven:
    - Preheat your oven to 350°F (175°C). Grease a mini muffin tin or line it with mini paper liners.
2. Melt the Butter:
    - In a microwave-safe bowl or on the stovetop, melt the butter until it's completely melted and smooth.
3. Mix Wet Ingredients:
    - In a large mixing bowl, combine the melted butter with the granulated sugar. Stir until well combined.
    - Add the eggs and vanilla extract to the butter-sugar mixture. Beat until smooth and creamy.
4. Add Dry Ingredients:
    - Sift the cocoa powder, all-purpose flour, salt, and baking powder into the wet ingredients. Mix until just combined. Be careful not to overmix.
5. Fold in Mix-Ins (Optional):
    - If desired, fold in chocolate chips, nuts, or other mix-ins of your choice into the brownie batter.
6. Fill Mini Muffin Tin:
    - Spoon the brownie batter into the prepared mini muffin tin, filling each cup about two-thirds full.
7. Bake:
    - Place the mini muffin tin in the preheated oven and bake for 10-12 minutes, or until the brownie bites are set and a toothpick inserted into the center comes out with a few moist crumbs.
8. Cool and Serve:
    - Allow the brownie bites to cool in the muffin tin for a few minutes, then transfer them to a wire rack to cool completely.
9. Enjoy:

- Serve the brownie bites at room temperature. They can be enjoyed on their own or topped with a dusting of powdered sugar, a drizzle of chocolate ganache, or a dollop of whipped cream.

Tips:

- Mini Muffin Tin Size: If you don't have a mini muffin tin, you can use a regular muffin tin, but adjust the baking time accordingly.
- Storage: Store leftover brownie bites in an airtight container at room temperature for up to 3 days, or in the refrigerator for longer freshness.
- Variations: Get creative with your brownie bites by adding different mix-ins such as chopped nuts, chocolate chips, caramel pieces, or shredded coconut.

These brownie bites are perfect for parties, potlucks, or any occasion where you want a bite-sized chocolate treat. Enjoy their rich, fudgy goodness in every bite!

Taco cups

Ingredients:

- 1 pound ground beef or turkey
- 1 packet (about 1 ounce) taco seasoning mix
- 1/2 cup water
- 1 can (15 ounces) refried beans
- 1 cup shredded cheese (cheddar, Monterey Jack, or Mexican blend)
- 24 wonton wrappers
- Optional toppings: diced tomatoes, sliced black olives, diced onions, diced avocado, sour cream, salsa, chopped cilantro

Instructions:

1. Preheat the Oven:
    - Preheat your oven to 375°F (190°C). Lightly grease a muffin tin with cooking spray or oil.
2. Cook the Ground Meat:
    - In a large skillet, cook the ground beef or turkey over medium heat until browned and cooked through, breaking it apart with a spatula as it cooks.
    - Drain any excess grease from the skillet.
3. Season the Meat:
    - Add the taco seasoning mix and water to the cooked ground meat. Stir well to combine. Cook for an additional 2-3 minutes, stirring occasionally, until the mixture is heated through and thickened.
4. Prepare the Wonton Cups:
    - Press one wonton wrapper into each muffin cup of the prepared tin, gently pressing it against the sides and bottom to form a cup shape.
    - Place a teaspoon of refried beans into the bottom of each wonton cup.
5. Layer the Ingredients:
    - Spoon a tablespoon of the cooked taco meat mixture into each wonton cup on top of the refried beans.
    - Sprinkle shredded cheese over the taco meat in each cup.
6. Bake:
    - Place the muffin tin in the preheated oven and bake for 10-12 minutes, or until the wonton wrappers are golden brown and crispy, and the cheese is melted and bubbly.
7. Serve:
    - Remove the taco cups from the oven and let them cool in the muffin tin for a few minutes.
    - Carefully remove the taco cups from the muffin tin and transfer them to a serving platter.
    - Garnish with your favorite toppings such as diced tomatoes, sliced black olives, diced onions, diced avocado, sour cream, salsa, and chopped cilantro.

8. Enjoy:
    - Serve the taco cups warm as a delicious appetizer, snack, or part of a meal. Enjoy their crispy texture and flavorful filling!

Tips:

- Customize Fillings: Feel free to customize the taco cups with your favorite fillings. You can add or omit ingredients based on your preferences.
- Make-Ahead: You can assemble the taco cups ahead of time and refrigerate them until ready to bake. Just be sure to adjust the baking time accordingly if baking them directly from the refrigerator.
- Double Batch: This recipe can easily be doubled or tripled to feed a crowd for parties or gatherings. Simply adjust the quantities of ingredients accordingly.

These taco cups are a fun and easy way to enjoy the flavors of tacos in bite-sized portions. They're perfect for serving at parties, game days, or as a quick and tasty snack!

Mini pretzels with cheese dip

Ingredients:

For Mini Pretzels:

- 1 ½ cups warm water (110°F to 115°F)
- 1 tablespoon granulated sugar
- 2 teaspoons active dry yeast
- 4 cups all-purpose flour
- 1 teaspoon salt
- 1 large egg, beaten (for egg wash)
- Coarse sea salt (optional, for topping)
- Cooking spray or melted butter, for greasing

For Cheese Dip:

- 1 tablespoon unsalted butter
- 1 tablespoon all-purpose flour
- 1 cup whole milk
- 2 cups shredded cheddar cheese
- 1 teaspoon Dijon mustard (optional)
- Salt and pepper to taste

Instructions:

Making Mini Pretzels:

1. Activate the Yeast:
    - In a large mixing bowl, combine warm water, sugar, and yeast. Let it sit for about 5-10 minutes until the mixture becomes frothy.
2. Make the Dough:
    - Add flour and salt to the yeast mixture. Mix until a dough forms.
    - Knead the dough on a lightly floured surface for about 5 minutes until it becomes smooth and elastic.
3. Rise the Dough:
    - Place the dough in a greased bowl, cover it with a clean kitchen towel, and let it rise in a warm place for about 1 hour until it doubles in size.
4. Shape the Pretzels:
    - Preheat the oven to 425°F (220°C). Line a baking sheet with parchment paper.
    - Divide the dough into small pieces and roll each piece into a thin rope. Twist each rope into a pretzel shape.
5. Bake the Pretzels:
    - Place the pretzels on the prepared baking sheet. Brush each pretzel with beaten egg wash and sprinkle with coarse sea salt, if desired.
    - Bake in the preheated oven for 10-12 minutes until golden brown.

Making Cheese Dip:

1. Prepare the Roux:
    - In a saucepan, melt butter over medium heat. Add flour and whisk continuously for about 1-2 minutes until the mixture turns golden brown.
2. Add Milk:
    - Gradually pour in the milk while whisking constantly to prevent lumps from forming. Cook until the mixture thickens, about 2-3 minutes.
3. Melt Cheese:
    - Reduce the heat to low. Add shredded cheddar cheese to the saucepan, stirring until the cheese is completely melted and the sauce is smooth.
4. Season and Serve:
    - Stir in Dijon mustard, if using, and season the cheese dip with salt and pepper to taste.
    - Transfer the cheese dip to a serving bowl.

Assembly:

1. Serve:
    - Arrange the freshly baked mini pretzels on a serving platter alongside the cheese dip.
    - Enjoy the warm mini pretzels with the creamy cheese dip!

Tips:

- Variations: Experiment with different types of cheese for the dip, such as Monterey Jack, pepper jack, or Swiss, for unique flavors.
- Storage: Store any leftover mini pretzels in an airtight container at room temperature for up to 2 days. Reheat them in the oven before serving. The cheese dip can be stored in the refrigerator for up to 3 days and reheated gently on the stovetop or in the microwave.

Edible cookie dough bites

Ingredients:

- 1 cup (2 sticks) unsalted butter, softened
- 1 cup packed light brown sugar
- 1/2 cup granulated sugar
- 2 teaspoons vanilla extract
- 2 cups all-purpose flour
- 1 teaspoon salt
- 1 cup mini chocolate chips
- Optional: Additional mix-ins such as chopped nuts, M&M's, or sprinkles

Instructions:

1. Cream Butter and Sugars:
    - In a large mixing bowl, cream together the softened butter, brown sugar, and granulated sugar until light and fluffy.
2. Add Vanilla Extract:
    - Stir in the vanilla extract until well combined.
3. Incorporate Dry Ingredients:
    - Gradually add the all-purpose flour and salt to the butter-sugar mixture, mixing until fully incorporated and a smooth dough forms.
4. Fold in Chocolate Chips:
    - Gently fold in the mini chocolate chips (and any additional mix-ins, if using) until evenly distributed throughout the cookie dough.
5. Shape into Bites:
    - Using a small cookie scoop or spoon, portion out the cookie dough and roll it into bite-sized balls. Place the dough balls on a baking sheet lined with parchment paper or wax paper.
6. Chill:
    - Place the baking sheet of cookie dough bites in the refrigerator to chill for at least 30 minutes. Chilling the dough will help it firm up and make it easier to handle.
7. Serve:
    - Once chilled, the edible cookie dough bites are ready to enjoy! Serve them as a delicious snack or dessert.

Tips:

- Store: Store any leftover edible cookie dough bites in an airtight container in the refrigerator for up to 1 week. Alternatively, you can freeze the dough balls for longer storage and enjoy them straight from the freezer.
- Customize: Feel free to customize the edible cookie dough by adding your favorite mix-ins such as chopped nuts, M&M's, sprinkles, or peanut butter chips.

- Serve: These cookie dough bites are perfect for serving at parties, gatherings, or as a fun treat for kids and adults alike. Enjoy them straight out of the refrigerator for a cool and satisfying snack!

Cotton candy

Ingredients:

- Granulated sugar
- Food coloring (optional)
- Flavored extracts or oils (optional)

Equipment:

- Cotton candy machine

Instructions:

1. Preparation:
    - Before you start making cotton candy, assemble your cotton candy machine according to the manufacturer's instructions.
    - Place a large bowl or tray under the machine's spinner to catch the cotton candy.
2. Prepare the Sugar:
    - Pour granulated sugar into a clean, dry bowl. You can add a few drops of food coloring for colored cotton candy or flavored extracts or oils for flavored cotton candy. Mix well to distribute the color or flavor evenly throughout the sugar.
3. Start the Machine:
    - Turn on the cotton candy machine and let it preheat according to the manufacturer's instructions. It usually takes a few minutes for the spinner to reach the right temperature.
4. Spin the Sugar:
    - Once the machine is preheated, carefully pour a small amount of prepared sugar into the center of the spinner as it's spinning.
    - Use a cotton candy cone or a stick to catch the cotton candy as it forms. Hold the cone or stick at a slight angle and move it around the spinner to collect the cotton candy strands.
5. Continue Spinning:
    - Continue adding sugar to the spinner and collecting the cotton candy until you've made as much as you desire.
6. Serve:
    - Once you've finished spinning the cotton candy, transfer it to serving cones or containers.
    - Enjoy your homemade cotton candy immediately, as it's best enjoyed fresh!

Tips:

- Experiment with Flavors and Colors: Get creative by experimenting with different flavors and colors of cotton candy. You can use flavored extracts or oils to add unique flavors, and food coloring to create vibrant colors.

- Storage: Cotton candy is best enjoyed fresh, but you can store any leftovers in an airtight container at room temperature for up to a day. Keep in mind that cotton candy can become sticky and lose its fluffy texture if exposed to humidity.
- Safety Precautions: Be careful when working with hot sugar and a spinning machine. Follow all safety guidelines provided by the manufacturer of your cotton candy machine, and supervise children closely when making cotton candy.

Enjoy making and eating your homemade cotton candy! It's a fun and nostalgic treat that's perfect for parties, carnivals, or anytime you're craving something sweet and fluffy.

Veggie sushi rolls

Ingredients:

- Sushi rice (1 cup uncooked rice)
- Nori seaweed sheets
- Assorted vegetables (such as cucumber, avocado, carrots, bell peppers, and asparagus), thinly sliced or julienned
- Soy sauce, for serving
- Pickled ginger, for serving
- Wasabi, for serving
- Rice vinegar (for seasoning the sushi rice)
- Sugar (for seasoning the sushi rice)
- Salt (for seasoning the sushi rice)

Instructions:

Preparing the Sushi Rice:

1. Rinse the Rice:
    - Rinse the sushi rice under cold water until the water runs clear. This helps remove excess starch and prevents the rice from becoming too sticky.
2. Cook the Rice:
    - Cook the rinsed rice according to the package instructions, using slightly less water than usual to achieve a slightly firm texture. Once cooked, let the rice cool slightly.
3. Season the Rice:
    - In a small bowl, mix together rice vinegar, sugar, and salt until the sugar and salt dissolve. Gently fold this mixture into the cooked sushi rice until well combined. Let the seasoned rice cool completely before using.

Assembling the Veggie Sushi Rolls:

1. Prepare the Work Surface:
    - Lay a bamboo sushi rolling mat on a clean work surface. Place a sheet of nori seaweed shiny side down on the mat.
2. Spread the Rice:
    - With moistened hands, spread a thin layer of sushi rice evenly over the nori, leaving about 1 inch of space at the top edge.
3. Add the Veggies:
    - Arrange your choice of thinly sliced or julienned vegetables horizontally across the rice, about 1 inch from the bottom edge of the nori sheet.
4. Roll the Sushi:

- Using the bamboo mat as a guide, tightly roll the sushi away from you, starting from the bottom edge and rolling towards the top edge. Apply gentle pressure to shape the roll as you go.
5. Seal the Roll:
    - Moisten the top edge of the nori sheet with a little water to help seal the roll. Continue rolling until the entire roll is sealed.
6. Slice the Roll:
    - Use a sharp knife to slice the sushi roll into individual pieces, wiping the knife clean between cuts to ensure clean slices.
7. Serve:
    - Arrange the veggie sushi rolls on a serving platter and serve with soy sauce, pickled ginger, and wasabi on the side for dipping.

Tips:

- Variations: Feel free to get creative with your veggie sushi rolls by adding ingredients like tofu, tempura vegetables, or even fruit like mango or strawberries for a unique twist.
- Prep Ahead: You can prepare the sushi rice and slice the veggies ahead of time to make assembly easier when you're ready to roll.
- Practice Makes Perfect: Rolling sushi can take a bit of practice, so don't worry f your first few attempts aren't perfect. With practice, you'll get better at rolling tight and evenly-shaped sushi rolls.

Enjoy making and eating your homemade veggie sushi rolls! They're a healthy and delicious option for sushi lovers and vegetarians alike.

Chocolate chip cookie cups

Ingredients:

- 1 cup (2 sticks) unsalted butter, softened
- 1 cup granulated sugar
- 1 cup packed light brown sugar
- 2 large eggs
- 1 tablespoon vanilla extract
- 3 cups all-purpose flour
- 1 teaspoon baking soda
- 1/2 teaspoon salt
- 2 cups semisweet chocolate chips
- Optional: Mini muffin tin or regular muffin tin, cooking spray or cupcake liners

Instructions:

1. Preheat the Oven:
    - Preheat your oven to 350°F (175°C). If using a mini muffin tin or regular muffin tin, grease the cups with cooking spray or line them with cupcake liners.
2. Cream Butter and Sugars:
    - In a large mixing bowl, cream together the softened butter, granulated sugar, and brown sugar until light and fluffy.
3. Add Eggs and Vanilla:
    - Beat in the eggs one at a time, then add the vanilla extract and mix until well combined.
4. Incorporate Dry Ingredients:
    - In a separate bowl, whisk together the all-purpose flour, baking soda, and salt. Gradually add the dry ingredients to the wet ingredients, mixing until just combined.
5. Fold in Chocolate Chips:
    - Gently fold in the semisweet chocolate chips until evenly distributed throughout the cookie dough.
6. Form Cookie Cups:
    - If using a mini muffin tin, scoop a small amount of cookie dough into each muffin cup, filling them about two-thirds full. If using a regular muffin tin, scoop a larger amount of dough into each cup, filling them about halfway full.
7. Bake:
    - Place the muffin tin(s) in the preheated oven and bake for 10-12 minutes for mini cookie cups or 12-15 minutes for regular-sized cookie cups, or until the edges are lightly golden brown.
8. Create Indentations:
    - As soon as the cookie cups come out of the oven, use the back of a teaspoon or a small shot glass to gently press down in the center of each cookie cup to create an indentation. This will create a space for the filling.

9. Cool:
    - Allow the cookie cups to cool in the muffin tin(s) for a few minutes, then transfer them to a wire rack to cool completely.
10. Fill and Serve:
    - Once the cookie cups are completely cool, fill the indentations with your favorite fillings such as frosting, chocolate ganache, pudding, or whipped cream.
    - Serve the chocolate chip cookie cups as a delicious treat for parties, gatherings, or any time you're craving a sweet and satisfying dessert!

Tips:

- Variations: Get creative with your cookie cups by adding different mix-ins such as chopped nuts, dried fruit, or candy pieces to the dough.
- Storage: Store any leftover cookie cups in an airtight container at room temperature for up to 3 days. You can also freeze the cookie cups (unfilled) for longer storage, then thaw and fill them as needed.
- Customize Fillings: Experiment with different fillings to suit your taste preferences. You can fill the cookie cups with frosting, caramel sauce, Nutella, peanut butter, or any other filling you like.

Enjoy these delightful chocolate chip cookie cups, perfect for satisfying your sweet tooth!

Jellybean popcorn

Ingredients:

- 8 cups popped popcorn (about 1/2 cup unpopped kernels)
- 1 cup jellybeans (assorted colors and flavors)
- 1/2 cup unsalted butter
- 1 cup granulated sugar
- 1/4 cup light corn syrup
- 1/2 teaspoon vanilla extract
- 1/4 teaspoon salt
- Optional: Sprinkles or colored sugar for decoration

Instructions:

1. Prepare the Popcorn:
    - Pop the popcorn using an air popper or stovetop method. Transfer the popped popcorn to a large mixing bowl, removing any unpopped kernels.
2. Add Jellybeans:
    - Mix the jellybeans into the popped popcorn, ensuring they are evenly distributed throughout the bowl. You can use assorted colors and flavors to add variety to the snack.
3. Make the Syrup:
    - In a saucepan, melt the unsalted butter over medium heat. Add the granulated sugar and light corn syrup, stirring until the sugar is dissolved.
4. Cook the Syrup:
    - Bring the mixture to a boil, then reduce the heat to low and simmer for 3-4 minutes, stirring constantly. The mixture should thicken slightly.
5. Add Flavorings:
    - Remove the saucepan from the heat and stir in the vanilla extract and salt. Mix until well combined.
6. Coat the Popcorn:
    - Pour the hot syrup over the popcorn and jellybeans in the mixing bowl. Use a spatula or wooden spoon to gently toss the mixture until the popcorn and jellybeans are evenly coated with the syrup.
7. Cool and Serve:
    - Spread the coated popcorn and jellybeans onto a parchment-lined baking sheet or a large serving platter in a single layer.
    - Allow the mixture to cool and the syrup to harden before serving. You can speed up the process by placing the baking sheet in the refrigerator for about 10-15 minutes.
8. Optional Decoration:
    - If desired, sprinkle colored sugar or decorative sprinkles over the popcorn for added color and sweetness.
9. Serve:

- Once the popcorn and jellybeans are completely cooled and the syrup is hardened, break the mixture into clusters and transfer to a serving bowl or individual bags.
- Enjoy the sweet and crunchy treat as a fun snack for parties, movie nights, or any occasion!

Tips:

- Assorted Flavors: Experiment with different flavors of jellybeans to create a unique taste experience. You can use classic fruity flavors or try specialty flavors for added variety.
- Storage: Store any leftover jellybean popcorn in an airtight container at room temperature for up to 3 days. Be sure to keep it away from moisture to maintain its crunchiness.
- Customize: Feel free to customize the recipe by adding other mix-ins such as chocolate candies, nuts, or dried fruit for additional texture and flavor.

Enjoy this colorful and tasty jellybean popcorn, perfect for satisfying your sweet cravings with a fun twist!